KEEP CALM AND MOMMY ON

KEEP CALM AND MOMMY ON

dr tanu shree singh

duckbill

An imprint of Penguin Random House

DUCKBILL BOOKS

USA | Canada | UK | Ireland | Australia
New Zealand | India | South Africa | China | Singapore

Duckbill Books is part of the Penguin Random House group of companies whose addresses can be found at global.penguinrandomhouse.com

Published by Penguin Random House India Pvt. Ltd
4th Floor, Capital Tower 1, MG Road,
Gurugram 122 002, Haryana, India

Penguin Random House India

First published by Duckbill Books 2017

This edition published in Duckbill Books by Penguin Random House India 2020

10 9 8 7 6 5 4 3

ISBN 9789383331826

Typeset by PrePSol Enterprises Pvt. Ltd.

Printed at Repro India Limited

www.penguin.co.in

MIX
Paper from responsible sources
FSC® C047271

This is a legitimate digitally printed version of the book and therefore might not have certain extra finishing on the cover.

Contents

Confessions of a Not-so-super Mom

'You are doing such a wonderful job with the boys! You are a Supermom!'

Every time I hear that, I glance over my shoulder to make sure that I am the one being referred to. I usually brush it aside with a nervous smile. I do not have to think deeply to figure out whether or not they are wrong; I know they are. What's worse, I seem to be misleading people. I feel it is time I set the record straight: I am not a perfectly balanced, calm mother, who knows the perfect technique to make sure her kids turn out well.

There is a faint hope that my kids *will* turn out well—yes. But there is also a real possibility that they will not develop that halo of goodness around them.

There are days when all such hope seems lost; days that start with grunts and growls, and end in tears. The older one, Ishaan, towers over me, and the younger one, Vivaan, is steadily getting there. So it is slowly transforming into a battle of wits. And in a battle, the odds aren't exactly in your favour when the opposition gangs up. There are tears, sometimes. And elaborate rants to the man who treads with extreme caution at such times. I am not at my best then. I do not have a ready checklist of things to do in order to turn the situation around. At times, I hide out on the balcony, and let my dogs sit in my lap. At others, there are the unfortunate friends who get their heads chewed up over cups of coffee.

The issues vary:

- Grunts for a good morning
- Sibling wars. More like annihilation bids.
- Aversion to homework or anything remotely academic.
- First reading rights for books. Bloodshed is narrowly averted every time.
- Spikes in levels of the teenage rudeness hormones.
- Food preferences—one hates peas, the other loves them, and many more such lovely conflicts.
- Losing interest in paid-for classes the moment the receipt is received. Always.

This list can go on endlessly.

When I was a kid, my friend and I would collect velvet bugs, which were found in abundance every time it rained. We would take a jar and put in as many of these bugs as we could see. One day, we had collected over a hundred bugs. We carried the jar to a friend's house, and started walking up the stairs to her room. As fate would have it, the jar slipped from my hands and shattered with a loud crash. There were bugs on every step. The two of us tried very hard to catch them and put them back in another jar, but it was impossible. As soon as one was returned to the jar, we'd find another five taking off. Ten minutes later, we were sitting on the steps and crying, bugs scurrying off in all directions possible, and a horrified mother glaring at us from the bottom of the stairs.

That is exactly what motherhood seems like sometimes—velvet bugs scattering from a broken jar.

At such points, I question my mothering skills, doubt everything there is to doubt, and ponder every negative aspect of the cosmos.

See? Not perfect. Not a Supermom.

Once I am done wallowing in self-doubt, I start working on a comeback plan. It takes work, patience, chocolate, and sometimes days of immense focus. Ammunition is carefully selected and deployed. Sometimes peace talks work. Sometimes negotiations. And sometimes, it is war. There is only one ground rule—no violence.

'But your writings reflect complete control!' a friend I was having coffee with said.

'They do? Damn!' I nearly choked on my coffee.

I am a lot of things, but 'in control' has seldom been a part of the list. When I am writing, it is after the last wisp of battle smoke has been blown away. Then analysis helps to figure out what helped. It is not as if I saunter into the war zone carrying a clipboard with a ready to-do list.

Does having a PhD in Positive Psychology (that is a real subject, not me trying to make myself sound cheerful) give me extra advantage? Not really. The theories we learn are mercilessly twisted by each child that we bear. No research report works. Anger doesn't work. Inner-cheek-gnawing, teeth-clenching patience, however, does. And there is no cape. I wish there was.

The next time you see a doting mother talking softly to her children, who look like tiny angels, know this—she has her bad moments too, and the angels can easily sprout horns like the devil. If she seems Supermom-like, then her kids' teenage hormones have not kicked in, or she is great at putting up a façade, or they are all just recovering from a battle.

The next time you see a dishevelled woman downing an extra-strong coffee, with two kids staring at her, their faces set in a scowl, pat yourself on the back and feel better. You are not her today. For now, you're a Supermom.

I try to learn as much as I can, and mostly try not to lose it. And if I succeed in not getting reduced to a bundle of nerves, in not planting a slap across the two teenaged faces, and in containing my self-doubt, that's not a bad day. I am a mum, a human one, not a Supermom with a solution to every problem. The experiences I share are in the hope that some mum somewhere would find them useful.

My life revolves around two boys, but this book is for parents of both, girls and boys. I dislike using 'they' when referring to children because being a good parent is all about reacting to each child as an individual. I have therefore used 'he' and 'she' fairly indiscriminately in the book, though I have tried not to change the child's gender in the course of a paragraph.

WE AND THE WORLD

Dealing with Diversity

Some years ago, Vivaan alighted from the school bus with a horrified look on his face. He dived right in.

'Did you know that Indians are shot the moment they land in Pakistan?'

'WHAT? Who the he—! Who told you that?'

'My friend. He said his father told him. I am never ever going there.'

After the 2014 massacre in a school in Peshawar, Vivaan came back looking shattered. 'Some kids were discussing the gory images they saw, Ma. They say that they don't care, because it was in Pakistan.' All of ten years and already prejudiced.

Prejudice starts colouring children's vision much earlier than we as parents would like. If it is not based on nationality, it could be religion, colour of skin, economic conditions, or simply whether or not one wears glasses. The boys have come home in tears because they got called 'four-eyed' or 'nerds' because of their glasses. They constantly tell me about kids being nasty for the most trivial reasons—from grades to the braces they have to wear. Childhood is an age of innocent cruelty. Spend a day at school and you'd hear the nastiest words being hurled around without the children even knowing what they mean.

Children are not born prejudiced but they pick it up fairly quickly. In a recent study on how children learn about prejudice, Sonia Kang and Michael Inzlicht of the University of Toronto concluded that for a six-year-old, one of the most powerful educational tools might be direct instruction.[1] Scientists found that as children get closer to the age of ten, they begin to rely more on their own experiences rather than what people tell them. But for younger kids, instruction trumps experience.

In other words, the six- and seven-year-olds take an adult's word at greater value than they do their own nasty experiences. The results showed that young children's 'expectations about experiencing prejudice will be shaped by the beliefs that are communicated to them by adults'. Kang says, 'The expectations that are established in early childhood are likely to form the building blocks for beliefs about stigmatisation later in life.'

When you tell your child that he should stay away from the maid's son since he is a 'bad boy', you are preparing him for a lifetime of contempt towards people who are not as well-off as he is. When, at a restaurant or a mall, you giggle on seeing an obese man and point him out to the kids, you are creating another monster about body image, and telling them that being fat is funny. The next thing you know, they have nicknames for the fat kid in their class. Do we really want our children to grow up to force people into small boxes based on biased beliefs? Absolutely not.

However, it would be foolish to expect your kids to grow up without being plagued by any prejudice, or without forming stereotypes. Even if they get a positive environment at home, we live in a society that discriminates on the basis of their skin colour, religion and caste, among others, and nurtures prejudice in every generation.

In the increasingly diverse world we inhabit, we share spaces with people different from us in our colonies, schools and workplaces. It has become even more imperative that children learn to respect diversity rather than close their minds to it.

So what can we do? Based on different studies, and my experience as a mother of two opinionated children, here are some things that do work:

HOW TO TEACH CHILDREN TO RESPECT DIVERSITY

Talk, talk, and some more talk

When Vivaan, then three years old, came back from school one day and asked if his classmate was weird since his skin was much darker than his, we talked. When Ishaan said, 'I think girls are weak',—oh, did we talk!

There is a difference between talking to and talking down to. The idea is not to tell them that they are wrong but to help them arrive at that conclusion. Give them facts that are contrary to the bias in their heads. So, Vivaan and I sat and discussed people with different skin colours who excelled in what they did. His conclusion: 'I could be the colour of a rainbow and it wouldn't matter.' As for the elder one, I resisted smacking the back of his head for calling the super-species weak, and we talked instead, of family and friends, and how strength and gender had nothing to do with each other.

👍 Set an example

I know, that is a lot to live up to, but this is the extra baggage you have to live with if you are a parent. If you want them to emulate something, set an example. On the one hand, we, pious parents, lecture kids that all human beings are equal. But, on the other hand, on a trip to a restaurant with the maid, we send her off to a separate table, in a corner far from ours.

Setting the right example is crucial during the critical age of around five to eight years, as pointed out by Kang. They will absorb everything adults say or do.

Last month, Vivaan asked, 'Mum, do we have separate utensils for our helpers?'

'No. Why do you ask?'

'You know some kids in my class told me that they have separate stuff for the helpers. I find that very weird. How are they different from us? I think it is rude.'

It's a miniscule victory, but a triumph nevertheless.

👍 Understand where the question is coming from

Knowing the antecedents of a particular query can help in making kids understand the basis of the prejudice, and also in countering it. If something happened at school, first get the details of the incident, and then discuss it. Addressing the larger issue without going into details of the causes might make little sense to them. Talking in context helps.

👍 Pause and think

It is okay to tell your kids that you do not know the answer and need time to think about it, rather than say something, that unwittingly reflects your own bias. Sometimes, the questions they throw at us force us to face our own biases. At that point, it is a good idea to pause and reflect—am I right to hold that view? Do I want to pass it on to my children or would I want them to form their own opinions? When in doubt, talk to others or read before you tackle the issue.

👍 There will be hard questions—be prepared

Prejudice is not limited to race, religion or appearance. More uncomfortable issues, like sexual orientation, may sneak up, and hit you in the face when you are least prepared. Again, educate yourself. We have far too many prejudiced people out there and we can definitely do without more. So, before forming an opinion based on popular media or a stray statement by a friend, read extensively and broaden your mind.

👍 Literature to the rescue!

What can I say—I am biased towards books! There are a million books out there that effectively teach children to respect diversity and form informed opinions. Let them read religious texts, ethnic histories, and a wide variety of fiction. At the last World Book Fair, we picked up stories from the Quran and had a long discussion about them, much to the disapproval of a few people I used to know.

👍 Encourage them to mix

Whenever the opportunity presents itself, encourage them to interact and make friends with children from varied backgrounds. The park that the boys go to in the evening sees a mix of kids coming to play. Initially, the group that they played with had reservations about the guard's son playing with them. Eventually, the boys convinced the others that he was a good bowler, and hence integral to the team.

👍 Never lose heart

Despite saying the right things and doing the right stuff, there will come a time when you are left wondering where the negativity is coming from. Don't lose heart and never question your parenting. Deal with the situation independently, without taking it as a reflection on your skills or your child's goodness. The world out there is not necessarily sensitive, and children absorb all sorts of things from it. As long as we try to undo the damage, we are good.

As they grow older and form their own opinions, this list will change. A prejudice-free society is a thing of fables, but a positive outlook and compassion is definitely achievable. We always have a choice—do we want our kids to grow in an environment fraught with uncertainty and hatred, or do we want them to grab that faint glimmer of positivity and hang on to it? We have seen what negative biases can do to us; it is time to give the other side a fair chance.

Of Naughty Corners and Sparkly Stars

'Naughty corner, now!'

'Nooooo! Sorry. I'll never bite bhai again.'

'Now.'

That's how the conversation usually went about ten years ago when Vivaan was three. I don't exactly remember where I discovered this magical disciplining technique (along with a few other downright unscrupulous tricks), but I vividly remember how I got to the point.

Whoever thinks that tiny toddlers are only giggling bundles of joy is severely delusional, has an entourage of aayahs at her beck and call, or is bent on deluding unwary childless people. Sounds exaggerated? Think again.

Remember when the nights were an endless series of diaper changes and bawling children, and days were spent figuring everything else around sleep schedules of the little devils? Stuff like running a comb through your hair seemed like a luxury. I forgot how that felt for a long time—untangled hair that was tied neatly. Baths were hurried and meals even more so. If it is like that with a single child, compound that however many times by the fact that I have two sons, with an age difference of two years.

By the time Vivaan was two, I had sunk into delirium. The day was one endless cycle of fight, kick, cry, bite, repeat. I was required to be the referee or a shoulder to cry on, depending on the severity of the bite. Things got out of hand and I found myself screaming at them very frequently. It was effective for a while—not in solving the problem, but at least in shoving it under the carpet. And helping me let some steam off.

I couldn't be shouting myself hoarse for the rest of my life. I am not sure whether it was a penny, an apple or the other shoe that dropped, but something did. I realised it could not go on like this.

When a child makes a mistake and we shout or, in some cases, whack her, this is what we are doing:

WHEN YOU YELL AT YOUR CHILD, YOU ARE ...

Looking for a quick fix

A child won't dare to mess with a towering adult who is shouting at or smacking her. This is quickest possible solution—to scare her and shut her up, at least for the moment.

Providing a kid with a faulty problem-solving mechanism

'Shouting and hitting works for Mum and Dad, so it will work for me.' There—you have just created a bully, who might grow up to be an adult with skewed ideas of relationship management. When in a fight, shout and intimidate.

Damaging their self-concept

A young child's self-concept is more fragile than a delicate spider web. At the stage when she is still struggling to form a basic sense of self, if she gets subjected to physical or emotional violence, the healthy development of her self-concept may be jeopardised. The fine threads that hold everything together snap and the web ends in a messy tangle.

Living in denial

'Me? I never hit my children! Sometimes a whack or two but then what can you do? Karna padta hai.' Sounds familiar?

Most of us live in denial. We deny that we are overly strict, we deny that the slap had more to do with our own anger, and we deny that things might be out of our control.

Justifying our weakness

'I get blinded with rage and can't help hitting the little bugger! She just does not listen!' Well, you were unable to control your rage so it is your problem, not your child's. It is harder to take a step back, control the anger and then deal with the situation calmly. Easier, of course, to yell and slap.

Before you know it, you would have set a pattern. You yell at or hit the poor child, who, in response goes into a shell or worse—stops caring.

What can we do? We could continue to live in denial that we are doing the things listed above. We can reaffirm the belief that only the rod works. We can ridicule the idea that displaced aggression could have found a foothold in our lives. Or we could actually do something to change it.

Once I realised I needed to change things, I started looking for alternatives. Here is my list of dos and don'ts to add to the millions already out there. This is based solely on experience and desperate search for information over the years, and has absolutely nothing to do with the sleepy lectures on developmental psychology that I attended a few decades back.

HOW DO YOU DEAL WITH ANGER?

Realise you are not a god

Even gods have beheaded their children (and fixed an elephant's head in its place) in a fit of rage so spare yourself the torture! We are human and we cannot be right all the time. The sooner we admit our shortcomings, the closer we are to a solution. So stop telling yourself that you never lose it—the idea is to make sure we do not make a habit out of it.

Get out of the situation

After getting used to yelling and getting instant results, it gets difficult to resist the lure. So when anger strikes, promptly strike anger back. A glass of water, deep breaths, pacing around—whatever works. Gather yourself before the danger warning goes off. Give yourself a timeout. Whatever the crisis, it is better dealt with after splashing water on your face and washing away the rage.

Research, read or create

Look for alternative methods of disciplining. I found the idea of a naughty corner on one of the desperately searched sites and it worked wonderfully back then.

A rough guide to the duration of timeout is that it should be equal to the age of the child. So, say, if a three-year-old bites her older sibling, she sits in a chair facing the corner of the room for three minutes. The key to making it work is persistent consistency with clarity. Explain in a few short sentences why she needs to sit it out. A long speech never works. Even if the timeout doesn't seem to work at first, keep at it. Eventually it will.

👍 Try positive reinforcement

Though the naughty corner works, it doesn't mean that we get the poor kid to camp in the corner for eternity. It has to be a mix where the balance tips in favour of positive reinforcement. Reward specific behaviours. 'You have been a good girl today' is a generic statement. But saying 'It is great that you helped clean your toy bin today' has a far greater impact. She ought to know exactly what she is being praised or rewarded for.

👍 Try more positive reinforcement

Giving your child tokens/coupons/stars for displaying specific behaviours, which she can exchange at the end of the week for a book, or an activity, works wonders. In fact, Vivaan took to reading out of greed for tokens that he could then exchange for extra time at the park, or a scoop of ice cream.

👍 Reward but don't give the shop away

Rewards undoubtedly work and get kids to behave well. But the question is, what should be the exchange value of the tokens? Make a list of desirables. Start with the lowest value and gradually increase it. If, at the first instance, you throw a feast, it becomes hard to top that. Ultimately, the goal is to phase out these rewards and replace them with praise and applause and then finally, a drive from within the child to do things right.

👍 Pick your battles

Just as we are human, these seemingly devilish creatures are human too. They will be flawed, so don't harbour any ideas of an ideal child. That little person you have is ideal for you, complete with her faults. Accept them. Choose specific issues that urgently need to be dealt with.

For example, I was okay with my younger one not eating pumpkin stew but nearly scratching Ishaan's eyes out was entirely unacceptable.

👍 Every fire can be fought

The child comes home with a C—or let's say, an F—on a paper. What do you do? You can tell her she is a disgrace, she doesn't work at all and proclaim that she will end up being a failure. Or you could just gather the fire-fighting equipment required.

When we tell kids that bad grades are irreversible or that their bad behaviour defines their character forever, we are telling them that there is no hope. Instead, if we approach both successes and failures with equanimity, it gets easier for kids to cope with both the ecstasy of achievement and the gloom of defeat, and to look at 'What next?' rather than dwell on the past.

I have never claimed to be an authority on parenting but I can cite the sanity plea: it has been fifteen years and I am still sane. The tokens still work though the stakes have changed. I get to hear all their secrets (or so I would like to believe). We reason, argue and I still end up having my way without them suspecting a thing!

The best part is that they don't hide their blunders from me. After a little hesitation and some preliminary mumbling, they confess. Sometimes, I still go and splash water on my face; at other times only a full-body dunking works. From grades to fights, everything is discussed and dealt with—some with hugs and some with a timeout.

Yours Sincerely, Santa Claus

I am a Hindu, at least by birth. Practicing the religion is limited to a confused Diwali puja, reading bits of the Ramayana as a part of the Akhand Paath when I was a kid, and getting an information overload from Amar Chitra Katha. I do believe in God, but I definitely do not think of faith as monochromatic. I get disturbed when I see bids to allegedly 'protect religious identities' in the form of boycotting or decrying other religions.

We believe in Santa. Yes, the boys still do. At fifteen and thirteen years of age, they have elaborate conspiracy theories involving the dark side of the moon, Santa's time-stopping abilities, and his supersonic sleighs. Does that make me a Christian? Not any more than devouring bowls of halwa at Diwali makes me a true Hindu.

The month of December saw increased online activity in our household. I have this Santa email account that the boys write to, and that Santa uses to respond. Each evening, we hoodwink each other, or so we pretend, and write emails.

From almost figuring on the naughty list, to everything that they were grateful for, they write about it all. And though Santa has the whole world to cater to, he thinks that these two boys are special and require prompt replies.

I come across two kinds of naysayers:

One lot feels we are turning a blind eye towards our own rich heritage, and leaning towards the west. Their argument is that we may lose our own religious identity, and the boys will get westernised. I believe that email exchanges with Santa emphasise the power of good, make the children think back on the year, get them to figure out how to be better people, and spark their imaginations—and do not result in our centre of gravity being shifted away from where we are. Just because the boys are excited about Santa leaving half-eaten cookies, have promised to do good, and treat their mum like a goddess (yeah, Santa has that odd precondition), it doesn't make them roll their Rs or forget their roots. Believe me, with so many reminders around, they couldn't do that even if they wanted to.

The other lot thinks I am encouraging the kids to escape to imaginary worlds. The boys imagine themselves at Hogwarts when they read Harry Potter, make elaborate escape plans when they read dystopian literature, and shed secret tears when imaginary characters die. Oh, wait. Those are the characteristics of bookworms, not delusions. Believing in Santa does not lead to personality disorders. Don't take *my* word for it, there are people with volumes of research to back that claim.

Now coming to the larger question: why indulge them anyway? As parents, we somehow tend to measure everything by its usefulness. Does a book have a moral? If not, it is useless, and there is no need to read it. Does going for storytelling sessions increase my child's vocabulary to formidable levels? No? Bah. Do toys serve any purpose other than drain the pocket? Absolutely not.

What underlies this is that as parents, we are always trying to balance spending money with the benefits that the child gets in being better equipped at handling the competition ahead. There is nothing wrong in limiting how much you spend on your children: the problem lies in the focus on utility or tangible outcome.

The same logic applies to Christmas. We often complain that children believe in Santa only for the gifts, that Christmas has become a major commercial event, and what is the child learning anyway? If, as a parent, I am simply buying fancy gifts and giving in to demand lists, then yes, all my children are getting out of Christmas is organised greediness. But if somehow, it makes my kids understand that gifting is not just about receiving, if it brings joy and sharing and introspection at the end of the year, then I think the gifts are absolutely worth it.

The email exchanges that we have start with lists: 'Get me Lego or a Deadpool action figure', 'I need a telescope', and of course books. Santa replies with stories of Rudolph wanting to meet their pet dog, Dobby, and discusses the 'Christmas spirit'. The conversation veers to listing ten things they were really grateful for in the year gone by. The answers will stay close to my heart forever. Then, there is Santa's confused mail declaring that Evelyn, the accountant elf, insists that they had to be on the naughty list. Out tumble confessions and promises of being good. We ultimately settle for one gift each, and are also making a gift for the goddess since she is a good mum. These exchanges would seem nonsensical to most people.

Over the years, through these mails, the boys have talked about their good and bad times, their hopes and fears for the coming year, and their opinions on a few issues. For us, religion is more than idols, colours, gifts and rituals. It is about recognising good, fighting our own devils, and knowing we are never lonely. It is about being human.

Should Religion be a Choice?

'Do you not believe in god?' There was a fair amount of accusation in the teacher's voice.

'Eh?' I was expecting a detailed analysis, down to the fifth decimal place, of the percentage scored by the younger one, and definitely not a theological debate.

'Last week, during assembly, Vivaan refused to fold his hands, saying he doesn't believe in god. So I was wondering if you teach him ...'

'He has independent beliefs. That is his business, not mine,' I cut her short.

Reluctantly, she got back to the prescribed agenda of the parent-teacher meeting. It was evident that she didn't approve. I do not mind that. I have a fairly thick skin now.

But the question remains, why do we want children to have strong religious beliefs? Is it for inculcation of the right morals and values? Or to motivate the child to strive for achievement of the ideal self? Or for preserving our cultural identity? Whatever the reason, most of us force our religious ideas on children without giving them much opportunity to explore. No, I am not an atheist. But I also do not believe in forcing the boys to fold their hands in front of the idols.

A few years ago, I came across a question on social media: 'Is teaching religion to children at an age when they can get confused between dogma and morality not a form of child abuse?'[2] It might sound extreme, but give it a thought. After all, lack of specific religious education does not translate into lack of character strength in a child. On the contrary, exclusive focus on the beliefs and practices of a single religion to the exclusion of others, can be potentially more harmful than no exposure to any religion.

In December 2014, Vivaan came back from school broken-hearted after the chilling Peshawar massacre. One of his classmates had casually dismissed the killings as something that happened to Pakistani Muslims. My son has no religious education, and he came back in tears; the other child showed no empathy because it had happened to kids who were not of his faith.

I am sometimes accused of raising children with no religious identity. I do not see a problem with that.

I grew up in a home where my mum spent half her time trying to trace me in the neighbourhood, where I'd disappear to play in the evenings, and the other half trying to get me to study. She never told me to light an incense stick. So, it is her fault, really. Papa was mostly found hidden in the folds of the newspaper when he was home. Sundays were spent playing the game of Boggle in the weekend supplement. He taught me how to change electrical fuses, plugs, anything with wires, and to never come home crying. Yeah, he had a single rule—if you are in a fight, never come home crying. I rarely did.

My family failed miserably their task of moulding me into a Hindu, let alone the kind of insecure Hindu who is intolerant of others, wants every movie or book that dares to question the religion banned, never questions rituals, and dreams of converting the world. Every Diwali, my father fished out the forgotten aarti book and tried to figure out which prayer had to be sung. That was about the extent of our religious engagement when we were growing up.

My grandfather once stood in front of my grandmother's little altar at home, where she was praying to a million gods, and remarked, 'The poor gods must be elbowing each other for space and prasad.' He went for the Vaishno Devi trek with us since he wanted to walk the distance, but didn't enter the temple.

Since we have not embraced a single faith as the directive by which we live, the boys are curious about different religions, respectful of people regardless of their faith, and relentlessly question prejudices. Are these not important values for the generation that is coming of age in a world continuously being torn apart on religious lines?

There was a heated debate on TV recently about extremism and its links with religion. After everyone had screamed their two bits, Ishaan said, 'Mumma, at the hospital today, I saw this man spread out his prayer mat and pray. Am I supposed to view him with suspicion just because he is praying?' He has learnt to see people independent of their religion.

Ishaan once buried a dead lizard that his classmates were playing with and was ridiculed at school for weeks.

He didn't mind, for he believes 'being disrespectful to the dead is uncool'. He feels immensely grateful for his family and the privileges he has. Vivaan appreciates art, is caring towards other living things, rescues tadpoles from the school playground, and stands up for kids who are being bullied. Neither of them has ever touched a religious book for the purpose of inculcation of values. However, I can safely say that so far they come across as virtuous kids.

Vivaan says he might believe in god if he is given sufficient evidence. He has an elaborate theory about how god could be an alien. He loves to read up bits of history and science that indicate the presence of alien life. I am happy that he is curious about the world around him, and in trying to wrap his head around the concept of religion, he is learning a whole lot of new things. Because they are not forced to learn, they are curious about themselves and others.

I cringe each time I see self-appointed advocates of any religion spewing venom at others. I cringe because I can see the power games behind the divisive lines, I cringe because there is hatred splattered on each turn of the newspaper page, but mostly, I cringe at being able to see all this while most people remain blind. They see it as a bid to protect their religious identities. I see it as an attempt to stifle everything that is humane. They see the likes of me as hypocrites, traitors, blind sympathisers, and an embarrassment to our 'own' religion. I see us as what we should be—humans.

I should have been taught better. I should have asked the guy who delivered the pizza yesterday if he was a Hindu. The house painters should have been interviewed about their beliefs. A few winters ago, the woman who had rolled down her window to hurriedly give a blanket to a homeless man never bothered to ask his religion. Pshaw! I think the chap who used to drive the younger one's school bus back when he started school was of questionable faith. Blood donors should put in a clause about the religion of the victims who can receive their blood. Hell, we didn't even bother to find the preferred god of the injured guy we helped. Blasphemy. But you can't blame me—I was raised colour-blind. It is not my fault.

I got back home, all these thoughts still clouding my mind, when I heard a voice. 'How was the report?' Vivaan was waiting at the gate. They always do when I go for the dreaded PTA meetings.

I smiled and gave him a thumbs-up. The frown gave away to a smile and a huge sigh of relief.

'So why didn't you fold your hands during the prayer at assembly?' I asked him.

'Don't believe in god.'

'Hmm. Cool. Then no Santa either?'

The hug ended, and a pair of determined eyes stared at me.

'I don't know about god but Santa exists. He does.'

Ah, well. We do have a long way to go.

Building Resilience

I am less careful around the children now. They read newspapers; there isn't much I can do. They see images, read articles and shed tears.

One day, after school, Ishaan looked worried. 'Mum, has the Taliban leader said he is going to wipe out all the children of the world? My classmates said so.'

Vivaan asked, 'Can it happen in our school too?'

'Did any child survive?' Ishaan continued.

As I tried to explain as calmly as possible what had happened, I noticed that they were hanging on to each word. They were scared and seeking survival strategies. And going by conversations I had with other mums, so are most kids. And most grown-ups.

There will always be times when as parents, we would wish that newspapers were blank, and we could cocoon the little ones. But the information will always reach them. And more often than not, it would be fairly twisted when it comes from their trusted source—their friends at school.

What do we do? How do we heal the little ones? Do we give in to fears, often not unreasonable ones? Thankfully, leading psychologists believe that we can help children learn to be resilient. How do we promote resilience then?

HOW TO TEACH KIDS TO BE RESILIENT

Discuss in age-appropriate terms

When the boys were younger, they could still be somewhat shielded from the world. But now, at thirteen and fifteen, respectively, their knowledge of what is happening in the world has grown exponentially, and protecting them is tougher. It is always a good idea to inform them about whatever is going on by using words and facts appropriate for their age.

Listen

Do not brush aside your child's concerns and questions as ridiculous. They might seem meaningless from where we stand, but for them these are very real threats. Listen with attention. Then, without once calling it ridiculous, try to lay the fear to rest.

Discover your child's strengths

Being a Positive Psychologist, I am biased towards individual character strengths. Research shows that an individual who consciously exercises his strengths is happier and better adjusted.[3] The VIA survey offers various tests for different age groups to discover one's strengths.[4] If the child is too young for it, observe him. Know what gives him true happiness and encourage him to do that in times of stress. This obviously does not imply that if choclates give him happiness, buy him a bagful. It has to be something deeper.

👍 Stick to a routine

Routines are a great source of security and comfort. Make sure that in times of stress, the routine is maintained, from homework to bedtime story. Be there. The soothing presence of the parent goes a long way in healing.

👍 Find channels of communication

Vivaan tends to bottle up his emotions. He finds it easier to express himself in writing. Ishaan is very comfortable talking to his grandmother. I use these channels. I use the Santa email account to talk to the younger one, and Nani does a wonderful job of listening to the older one. The idea is for each child to have a place for airing his fears, and for us to help him deal with their anxieties.

👍 Do not be overprotective

Left to our instincts, as parents, we want to protect our kids from every scrape, nick and hurt. But this doesn't allow them to learn to heal. Let them have age-appropriate freedom. Let them face emotional lows, and then help them learn to cope. The process of being resilient to bigger, more real threats is learnt through fairly smaller hurts.

👍 Be honest

Vivaan's question—'Can it happen in our school too?'—echoed in my head for a long time. My instinct, in a futile bid to protect him, was to hug him and say, 'Of course not.' Instead, I said, 'It can happen anywhere. And so can many other things. But we can not let fear take over our lives, can we?'

Then a conversation followed about fears and assumptions. Saying that bad things cannot happen threatens our position as trusted adults. Being honest about the facts—possibly minus the gory, overwhelming details—is way more reassuring.

👍 Exercise emotional control

While watching the news, I often feel choked with rage. The parent's emotional reactions are cues for children to judge balance in their world. Whenever I was injured as a child, I remember feeling reassured on seeing my father's calm face and hearing his soothing voice as he cleaned the wounds.

If we break down, they break down. Maintain an honest and brave front in front of them. If you need to pretend, take time out, wash your face, talk to a friend, and then get back to donning that cape. This doesn't mean it's not okay to cry. However, don't cry when the child is already gripped by fear.

👍 Encourage expression

You do not always need to tell your children what has happened. Ask them.

After the Peshawar attack, the boys came back from school with all sorts of distorted facts. We started the conversation with my workplace and what people were saying about the attack. This gave them a starting point to share what they had heard. Then one by one, we threshed out fact from fiction. But not once did we say 'That's ridiculous' or 'No, that child was wrong'.

When little Alan Kurdi was washed up on a beach, having drowned when his family was trying to escape from Syria, we spoke about the pain—but also of wars and the havoc they create in children's lives.

👍 Observe

Sometimes, a child who is unable to cope with the stresses around may display changes in behaviour, such as sleep disturbance, excessive clinginess, changes in eating patterns, lack of concentration, and an overall darkening of mood. Any persistent changes that are observed, and cannot be attributed to natural growth should be taken seriously, and professional help should be considered. Resilience should never be assumed. Just because kids are young doesn't mean that they will automatically bounce back soon. If they do not, seek help.

Discuss safety measures

Each morning's paper is filled with individual stories of loss and survival. One morning, on our way to school, Ishaan asked, 'My friend told me that some children pretended to be dead and were saved. Is that true?' I nodded and resisted the urge to tell him that I'll set the world on fire if someone so much as thought of harming him. Because saying that would be misleading.

It is a good idea to strike a balance between real fear, practical safety measures and acceptance of the unknown. Whenever the boys read about disasters, we try and discuss what all we can do in case we get caught in a bad situation. Their fears are real, and knowing that there is always a chance is comforting. Research on the dos and the don'ts, and discuss them.

There will always be threats. We, as parents and individuals, can never let fear get the better of us.

The Forsaken Angels

Fifteen years ago, I had this bundle in my arms that kept everyone on their toes and me at my wit's end. Yet watching him sleep, his tiny fingers firmly wrapped around mine, was probably the most divine experience. It is such a natural instinct, no? Becoming a mum and falling head over heels in love with that little thing! To have your world completely tossed around by one tiny sneeze and get your tear glands working in overdrive at the first scratch from those tiny nails on that soft face.

Loving one's child is instinctive. Or is it?

On numerous visits to the adoption centre where my mother works, I have constantly been plagued by questions I don't seem to find an answer to. Those doors open up to an entirely different world, far removed from the cosy, protective one that we create around our kids. Those doors lead to hallways where shrill playful squeals echo. The hallways lead to rooms with rows and rows of cots and small beds. Tiny hands are visible from the doorway.

A closer look and there they are, rows and rows of cots with little girls, flailing their arms as if looking for warmth. Their families rejected them for being what they are—girls. Some of them were thrown in dustbins and have had half their faces eaten by stray dogs. Some have brain damage from being hurled into roadside bushes from moving cars. Yet they are the lucky ones, for at least they survived. Almost all of them have permanent scars in their hearts—of rejection and uncertainty.

It is said that there is some good in each heart. What possible good drove these people to toss aside these infants like waste pieces of meat at a butcher's? This is not human. I remember when my kids were infants, I didn't leave them alone for even a second.

We stay awake, forever vigilant to the real or imagined needs of the little ones. All of us have been there—spent sleepless nights with our babies in our arms. Then, how do parents find the darkness within themselves to leave these frail, few-hour-old babies by the roadside?

At the adoption centre, these girls grow up to wait—for their turn for love, for care, and for a forever home. They might play and prance around but one question is always on their minds: 'When will my mumma come?' Sometimes, they get angry when a parent comes to pick up another child. Tantrums to tears—nothing they can do will change the course of their lives. Some are lucky enough to find new homes. Some just wait forever.

I had first taken Vivaan to the adoption centre when he was eight. He had been moved to tears on seeing the little ones there.

'You wouldn't ever leave me na, Ma?'

'No, love. Never.' I wrapped my arms around him.

'What kind of parents were they?' He dissolved into sobs and I was left with the same question.

The same eight-year-old had been complaining about how unfair his life was since bhai got a new toy and he didn't.

I want to tell him what unfair truly means; it means not having a mum to complain to about trivial toys, not throwing tantrums about 'bad food'. Unfair is waiting for those doors to open, hoping to find a parent who would envelope them in a warm hug, but instead being greeted by hopelessness. Those kids face an unfair, empty life each day with a smile. They just wait for their turn in life. They wait for their chance at life.

But I let it pass .... How can an eight-year-old understand what even grown-ups cannot fathom?

Should Kids Read the Newspaper?

Before the 2014 school massacre at Peshawar, ten-year-old Vivaan read the children's newspaper to which we had subscribed. Since these newspapers rarely answered all his questions, and I didn't have all the facts and figures, he felt the need to graduate to adult newspapers.

And with this decision, the world in its ugliest form appeared at the breakfast table every morning for him.

Did I do wrong by letting him read? Should I have shielded him? I think not. We know that newspapers are as much an essential read as the prescribed textbooks or the lovely novels that a child devours, but most of us are perturbed by the content in them. So, how does one initiate them into reading the news? And, more importantly, why?

WHY SHOULD A CHILD READ NEWSPAPERS?

👍 For (reasonably) authentic information

Let's face it: Kids get to know whatever is happening around them. The only things we can try to control are the sources of information. When Vivaan came home and told me a bizarre story related to a terrorist attack, we sat and read the newspaper together. His information came from his friends, who deliver the news like a game of Chinese Whispers. Now, he is informed enough to correct them.

The choice is yours: Would you not have them know the truth rather than rumours, prejudiced conjectures and 'alternative facts'?

👍 As an aid to self-discovery

The news isn't limited to murders and rapes. There is science, sports, movies, fashion, literature—a whole spectrum of interests is covered. A child who regularly reads the newspaper simply knows more about the world, and is therefore more likely to discover where his passions lie, and what things affect him the most.

👍 To widen horizons

'If you want to become somebody, read newspapers regularly,' my father used to say. Nothing is as comprehensive as a good newspaper being read from page to page. Knowledge is power and newspapers are the easiest way to access it. This is especially important in an age of social media, when all forms of distorted information are easily accessible.

👍 To balance attitudes

We strive to give our children a balanced diet. However, when it comes to forming opinions and attitudes, we simply let our long-held views influence our child's mind.

When kids read extensively, chances of them forming views that are truly unique to them are higher. And in a world that is often swayed by opinions that are prejudiced or inadequately informed, a child who is well-informed, aware of opposing points of view and has some knowledge of the facts underlying opinions has a unique advantage.

Most of us know these benefits, but it is the perils that scare us. The pages filled with hatred, crimes and gore can get overwhelming for anyone irrespective of age. So how does one go about it?

HOW DO YOU INTRODUCE YOUR CHILD TO NEWSPAPERS?

Start with children's newspapers

Quite a few options are available, both online as well as offline. We started subscribing to one when Ishaan was around seven years old. The whole idea of having his own newspaper that he could read like a grown-up gave him a thrill, which was soon shared by Vivaan. Since the papers are meant for kids, the write-ups are age-appropriate. This proved to be a nice tool to get the boys to develop a routine around reading newspapers. The fact that it was a weekly feature prevented it from becoming too taxing.

At any point, when your child is ready, or—as it happened in Vivaan's case—there is involvement with an issue or an event in greater detail, you can move to regular newspapers.

Discuss

Just handing over the newspaper rarely helps. It is a good idea to discuss the things that the child reads, encourage her to tell you about whatever is happening in the world, and show appreciation when it is something you are not aware of.

The child will also come to you with questions. We need to make sure that we do not force our perspectives on them—though obviously one does share one's opinion. It is important to highlight that this is an opinion only, and therefore it is possible to have other opinions. The idea is to discuss the facts, and then encourage the child to form her own views.

Be open

Every once in a while the child will chance upon a mainstream newspaper, or overhear a television journalist discussing issues like rape, terrorism, malnutrition, and darker issues that we try to protect them from. It is essential that we openly discuss everything.

If your child asks about rape, tell her what it is. Shying from the topic never helps. Children will find out eventually. The difference is, as parents, we can use appropriate words and give them accurate information. On the other hand, if she tries to find out on her own, her sources might not only be inaccurate, but completely outlandish. Being open is tough, but the hesitation goes away after the first few talks. So be brave, and take the plunge.

Give freedom

This is perhaps the most important bit. Sometimes, in an effort to make sure that children are getting a balanced view of the world, we force the kids to read all the headlines and report back. Making it a chore will probably lead the child to develop an aversion to newspapers. Freedom to read whatever part she wants to is the correct way forward. As a child, I used to eagerly wait for the Sunday edition since it had a game of Boggle in it that I played with my father. So even if the child just wants to check out the cartoons or movie listings or random jokes—let her. Eventually, she will want to read more.

👍 Spike interest

The boys love science, so whenever there is an article about an interesting discovery, I put on a bit of a show. I get all excited, and ask them, 'Have you heard about the Large Hadron Collider? Seems pretty cool!' Or 'Did you see the pictures of the latest species of frog they discovered?' The enthusiasm is mostly contagious and they dive right in. By evening, they are usually way more informed than me. Mission accomplished.

👍 Make it interesting

At the start, building activities around the newspapers helps to generate interest. When the boys started with the children's newspaper, we planned a few activities around it:

a. Scrapbooking

Get a nice scrapbook, markers, glue stick and child-friendly scissors. Ask the child to cut out and stick one thing of interest from the newspaper every week. It could even be an advertisement: Do not cringe. For the longest time, all that Vivaan scrapbooked was Calvin and Hobbes comic strips from the newspaper! Gently direct them towards news articles, weather reports, or any other section that could be of interest to the child.

b. Scavenger hunt

Print or draw up a nice scavenger hunt sheet and put it up on your board or fridge. Every day, write the hunt-question of the day on it from the newspaper. It could be anything from naming a person, to the name of the trophy a team won. Every correct response will win the child a star. And you can decide what an x number of stars can be exchanged for. As far as possible, stay away from material gifts alone. An ice cream with Mumma is a better idea than, say, a toy in exchange for ten stars. Every alternate day, you can play it in reverse, where the child poses a question and you have to hunt for the answer.

c. Word hunt

Get a nice notebook that the child can make into a personal dictionary. The idea is for them to write a new word they find in the paper each day, along with its meaning. During the day, try to use that word as frequently as possible in your conversations with the child and encourage him to do the same. A few years ago, my younger one and I had a fairly absurd conversation just because we enjoyed using the word 'smithereens'.

Today, the boys discuss or at least try to wrap their heads around complex political and social issues. We try to listen without forcing our views down each other's throat. We also realise that reading one newspaper is not sufficient. It is far more important to read from multiple sources, and to keep our horizons wide enough to let snippets of information slip in. The news, after all, is what someone somewhere chose to print and not necessarily everything that is going on in the world.

It is a tough thing to do, and will probably put you in a spot quite a few times. There will be days when you are too tired to discuss global warming and its impact on the penguins or answer endless queries on religious fanaticism. We need to let them in; we need to let their questions get answered. We need to stop being the gatekeeper, and let the children read and discover.

KEEPING YOUR CHILD SAFE

He is just three! And he wants to see my penis!

At twelve, I could barely braid my own hair. And she's writing love notes?!

The son saw his seniors kissing in school! What the hell is going on?

...

A Million Shades of Grey

Sometimes I pretend to be in a parallel universe with no wormhole connecting me to the world where a fight just broke out between my two boys, both a cocktail of hormones, raging to claim supremacy, and establish control over toys and books. The strategy mostly works. But sometimes, fractures in the space-time continuum appear.

'Mum, a friend suggested that I check out a pornographic site,' Ishaan declared one random day a couple of years ago.

They know how to create a wormhole, and suck me right back into their world. He had a smile plastered on his face.

'And?'

'Nothing. Just telling you.'

'There is nothing else you want to ask?'

'I know what porn is, and I seriously have no interest.' He sighed and tried to sound as cool as a thirteen-year-old possibly could.

That was his way of getting my attention, and he promptly launched into his wishlist of books to be bought at an upcoming book festival. There were no gasps, no fear, no fidgeting and definitely no hesitation when he used the big, bad P-word. We have talked about the birds and the bees, and yes we have moved on to discussing the more scary beasts—pornography, alternate sexuality, gender sensitisation, and sexual assault.

Most parents, and nearly all teachers, shy away from discussing pornography. And if, god forbid, a child is caught watching or reading porn, he is made to feel like a social outcast who has committed the worst moral crime there is. There are many books and articles stating the importance of discussing porn and warning kids about its dangers, but none really teaches you how to handle a situation where your child stumbles upon a porn site, or is caught surfing the net for porn. So we devised our own way and so far, things have been fine. One just cannot decide to have 'the talk' one day. It is a process and there are some pointers that one needs to be mindful of:

HOW TO PROTECT YOUR CHILD FROM PORN

👍 Remember: Sex is normal; curiosity even more so

Chant this, read about it, gather data if you have to, but at the end of the day, treat sex the way it is—real and normal. An interest in sex is part of every adult's experience, and of every child's too. There is nothing immoral about a child being curious about sex. I must have repeated this to myself and others a million times, and yet, it is never enough. So chant some more.

👍 Be factual, not coy

Use facts. Stop calling a penis 'wee-wee', or the vagina 'su-su', or whatever nicknames you have come up with. They are normal body parts, and by being shifty or shuffling uncomfortably whenever an inevitable reference to 'it' comes up, we are telling the child to be ashamed of his or her body.

👍 Put checks in place

Children should not have a free run of the computer or other gadgets connected to the internet. If they are accessing the internet on any gadget, there are a quite a few monitoring apps available that can be installed to prevent them from accessing porn or other objectionable sites. Research and install them.

👍 Talk

Installing security apps doesn't mean the job is done. Internet access beyond home is out of our control. Therefore, it becomes important that we talk. Tell your child what porn is.

Recently the boys were given limited iPad privileges, which meant that they could access the internet. So, I discussed the perils that lurk out there, including porn sites.

👍 Be logical

Just telling them what porn is and that it is bad, doesn't serve the purpose. Give them a few reasons:

a. Watching porn can lead to addiction

A study has revealed that the effect of porn on the brain is similar to that of drugs.[5] It can be addictive, and lead to denial, lifestyle changes and overwhelming feelings of guilt and depression.

b. Sex is beautiful, porn distorts it

Look at Barbie. Do you think a real woman looks like that? Or, for that matter, superhero figures. Just as these distort the image of a real healthy person, porn distorts the idea of sex. Rather than connecting it with emotions, porn links sex primarily with gratification, and most of it glorifies objectification, especially of women. Tell them that.

c. Body image issues

Most people shown in those pictures or videos are a product of elaborate surgeries or photo manipulation. When a child sees them, the image distorts his expectations of himself and his future partners, giving way to feelings of inferiority.

👍 Teach respect

It is often women who are objectified in pornography. Watching porn normalises a world view where women are degraded, treated as objects, and on some level, shown to enjoy violence. Over time, it leads to considering women as inferior, thereby dehumanising them. If boys are taught to respect women from the very beginning, they might be more critical of porn.

In the end, it is not really a big deal. You will stumble upon dubious search histories, or a child staring at the Google homepage when you walk in unannounced. Gather your senses, stay calm and help tide them over this phase of growth, changes and discoveries. Sex is not pornographic or evil. We have to treat it like the meeting grounds of bodily functions and emotions. All we need to do is be there when the children need us, without judging them. Contrary to what we'd like to believe, this generation is not that different from ours: They are just more vulnerable thanks to the virtual world. It is our job to be the gatekeeper and the guide, but never the judge. Ever.

Of Birds, Bees, and the Whole Jungle

'Ma, what is moisture-bating?'

'Moisture what? Give me some context, dude.'

'There is this boy in our class. He ran out of the washroom crying. I saw a group of boys sniggering after him. They said they had caught him moisture-bating.'

The fact that I was driving when this conversation happened, and yet managed to reach home without a scratch makes me a stellar driver.

'You mean masturbating.'

'The boys said moisture ... anyway, what is masturbating?'

And so began yet another conversation on sex education.

The boy who had 'educated' Ishaan had also given him some pointers regarding 'moisture-bating'.

In addition to being a calm driver, I am also capable of controlling emotional displays. So, while I was laughing hysterically inside (and I did endlessly giggle about it in the evening with one of my friends), my face was serious. We launched into a discussion about the whole thing, the myths attached to it and the fact that those boys were downright nasty for making fun of him.

Later that evening, during a conversation with a fellow mum, I realised another disturbing fact. With the children's hormones kicking in, most of us have been reduced to a fidgety, nervous bundle. We know that the much talked-about 'talk' is required, but it does not come easy. Thoughts buzz and bumble around in our heads at dizzying speeds, making the words even more jumbled.

Parents are gradually opening up to the idea of sex education but we educate (or hope that the school will) with blinkers on—we talk to our children about sex and stop at that. Rarely have I come across people who openly discuss sexual orientation, gender identities and, well, moisture-bating.

What all should be talked about, then? And, more importantly, when? Some children are not interested in sex for a long time, some are simply shy. The truth is, words are difficult, but there are certain things that we do need to mention.

HOW TO TELL YOUR CHILD

Don't blame the stork

The first step to raising an aware child is to tell him the truth.

I remember Vivaan at the age of three asking where he had come from. Ishaan muttered something about him being found in a drain but I told him he had been in my tummy.

'So I came out of the belly button?' His eyes were wide with fascination.

'Nope. The doctor made an incision and took you out.' Thank god for a c-section.

Caesarean or not, find your words and say them. Do not let them believe that god sent them over with an angel or a stork.

👍 Use the correct names

Use the correct names for body parts and actions: penis, vagina, anus, having sex, masturbating. If you are matter-of-fact and not coy, the child will feel less awkward or inhibited in coming back to you with questions or clarifications. It will also make it easier for you to overcome your awkwardness, trust me!

👍 Stop shaming

If your toddler decides to do the full monty, or the preschooler forgets to put on important articles of clothing, do not make a fuss. Don't shame your child about modesty or body parts. Yes, they have to learn social norms about clothing, but that can be done without shaming.

Similarly, as kids grow older and reach the preadolescent stage, it is easy to embarrass them with references to body changes, or even things like height and weight. It is important to be aware of this, and not make any comments that might be interpreted as body-shaming, or remarks on behaviour or clothes that might make them self-conscious.

👍 Always answer questions

'What is this?' Vivaan asked, holding the instruction pamphlet from a box of tampons, a few years ago. No stories were cooked up. Facts were stated and he took it all surprisingly well.

Children come with built-in nervousness sensors. So when you discover the child getting curious about sex, or when he hurls the most inappropriate question at the most inopportune time, do not break into a sweat, blabber, distract, or worse, shoo them away. That does two things—gets them more curious, and makes sure that they do not come to you for answers. There will always be questions. Stay calm and state the facts. If it is the meaning of a 'bad word' that your child wants to know, read out the meaning from the dictionary, and tell them why it is a bad word.

Never let there be any guilt or ridicule

You have to hand it to me. When the 'moisture-bating' discussion happened, I didn't laugh my head off. A straight face, a matter-of-fact discussion and a non-condescending voice go a long way. Thoughts of sex, masturbation, and curiosity about pornography can create a strong sense of guilt that ultimately leads to lowered self-esteem and a nagging feeling of moral failure in your child. Throw away your moral outrage.

Books always work

Luckily, there are many good books that talk about hormonal changes, bodily differences and sex. Get them. Read yourself. Read to your children. If it doesn't come naturally to you, read aloud in private to get rid of your inhibitions. Never rush through the text the way school biology teachers do. Pause. Make eye contact. Answer questions. And then move on.

Recently, I read *Talking of Muskaan* by Himanjali Sankar, which spoke about homosexuality, the difficulty that the protagonist faces in coming out, the bullying she faces, and the dangers of adolescent emotional turmoil. Sometimes, the best non-fiction books, and the most understanding parents are not able to help a child come to terms with themselves or with the world around them. Fiction helps in such cases. That book became a starting point for me to talk to Ishaan. We discussed the book and correlated it with the real world. It was an eye-opener. There are many such books out there. Explore.

For Your Bookshelf

Mummy Laid An Egg by Babette Cole
Where Did I Come From? by Peter Mayle
It's Not The Stork!: A Book About Girls, Boys, Babies, Bodies, Families And Friends by Robie H. Harris
It's So Amazing!: A Book About Eggs, Sperm, Birth, Babies, And Families by Robie H. Harris
It's Perfectly Normal: Changing Bodies, Growing Up, Sex, And Sexual Health by Robie H. Harris
What's the Big Secret? Talking About Sex With Girls and Boys by Laurie Krasny Brown and Mark Brown.
"What's Happening to Me?" A Guide to Puberty by Peter Mayle, Arthur Robins
Period: A Girl's Guide to Menstruation by JoAnn Loulan and Bonnie Worthen
George by Alex Gino
Forever by Judy Blume
What We Saw by Aaron Hartzler
Speak by Laurie Halse Anderson
The Perks of Being a Wallflower by Stephen Chbosky
Every Day by David Levithan
Talking of Muskaan by Himanjali Sankar
And Tango Makes Three by Justin Richardson and Peter Parnell
The Great Big Book of Families by Mary Hoffman
Kiss by Jacqueline Wilson

There is no end to the discussion

Your child needs to understand how he or she is physically different from the other sex. Depending on the child's comfort level, tell him how babies are born. Don't be quick to pat your back once you have 'educated' your child about sex. You have taught them what sex is, what good touch-bad touch is, and you have taught them the importance of safe sex. You cannot—alas!—go back to putting your head in the sand, and pretending that the child is sufficiently grossed out to abstain for a long time.

They are as curious as they were, albeit a bit more informed now. From online safety to pornography, everything needs to be tackled. You will have to talk about masturbation, infatuation, love, curiosity, consent and sexuality.

👍 Talk, talk and more talk

When Vivaan accidentally stumbled upon a pornographic site, we talked about what it was, why it was there, and what harm it could do to a person. When Ishaan told me about his classmates jeering at another boy for being different and calling him gay, we talked. When they saw news articles on molestation and rape, we talked. Again, present facts. Our job is to help them cope with the truth, and not distract them with lies.

👍 Stay calm—it's just masturbation!

It is just sex. Let us not make it a matter of life and death or, worse, honour.

Masturbation is a fairly common practice with self-stimulation occurring in kids as young as five years. In fact, some researchers claim that some form of sexual behaviours are observed even in utero! The goal is to ensure a middle ground; either extreme—corrosive guilt or a persistent all-consuming habit—is unhealthy. Your teenager will always find some way to leave you stumped.

Gather yourself and redefine morality. What is important is that your child is a good human being, and with your help, will grow up to be truthful and sensitive. None of that is possible if the child is buried under guilt.

👍 Babies do grow up

I know that this is the most heartbreaking part of parenthood, but they do grow up. The awkward teenager who is waiting for his voice to crack is at the threshold of adulthood and is a seething cauldron of hormones. The sooner we acknowledge that, the less shocking it would be to discover him getting interested in things beyond superhero toys and Lego.

Always be aware of the issues that are central to the child's developmental stage. Never assume that your child is too innocent to think about all this. Innocence has nothing to do with sexual development.

Somehow, we blank out when a child steps into adolescence. We acknowledge the growth in terms of height, and playfully pull the child's ear when he stands next to us and tells us that he is taller, but we shuffle when we sense other changes. We have all been through it. However, despite the first-hand experience, it helps to read up about the changes that adolescence brings. This aids in shutting the tiny voice up that keeps telling us that he is just a baby!

👍 Be logical

There is no moral higher ground where teenage sexuality is concerned. Keep morals and religion out of it, and talk to your child logically about it. Acknowledge that it is perfectly natural to be attracted to another person. Talk about the pros and cons of being in a relationship before the two people involved are mature, and chances are that you'll have a teenager who can make sensible choices. Or learn from his mistakes and move on, rather than spending enormous amounts of energy and time hiding things from you.

👍 Accept poor choices

We have been telling our kids that it is important to make mistakes, that we learn from errors, and that failures are the stepping stones to success.

Now is the time to walk the talk. He is a teenager; he will make mistakes. We all did. Be calm. There will be heartbreaks, and there will be occasions when your child is caught red-handed doing something he and you have agreed is not acceptable.

I'd rather have the boys come and tell me about it. I'd rather offer them hot chocolate as they pour their hearts out. I'd rather not find out accidentally and then go in to a loop of recriminations: 'How could you? You should be focussing on your career!' For your child, the world has halted. It is up to us, the parents, to help set it back in motion.

There is no script that you can just read through and get over with. It is a process. If your kid comes back with more questions, you are doing the right thing, and using the right words. Although the choice of words is up to each one of us, the common thread is honesty. As long as we are true to them and to ourselves, they will come back, and there will always be lots to talk about.

Of course I have many fears. Fear of my boys experimenting with sex a little too early, fear of them being ridiculed somehow, fear of not being there to protect them. But I cannot let my fears interfere with their growth. Till now, we have managed to joke about the first traces of a moustache, heard the sore-throated teenager croak, and assured him that his voice isn't breaking yet, and yes, talked about moisture-bating.

Draw a Line. Now.

- Research in the US has found that one in six men have experienced abusive sexual experiences before the age of eighteen. This figure was based on incidents of physical contact in US and Canada.
- A 2007 survey in India pointed out that more than 53% of children in India are subjected to sexual abuse.
- Sexual abuse harms boys and girls in ways that are similar and different, but equally harmful.

It is not just about girls. It is not just about sexual abuse. It is about any kind of abuse. It is about drawing a clear, sharp line. Why should a teacher get away with pulling a child's ear, humiliating a child in the name of disciplining, discouraging a child verbally, or slapping a middle-schooler who was flying a paper plane in the corridor?

I find the conversations that I have with my boys disturbing. Every other day, they tell me about some boy either being beaten up or yelled at by a teacher. These kids do not report all this to their parents. And it is not limited to a particular school—I have come across incidents of abuse reported by kids from different schools, the various so-called sports academies and hobby centres.

Often, children do not protest. Some believe that they deserve the punishment. Many hesitate to tell their parents. If I were to go by the anecdotes related by my boys, nearly all children who do not tell their parents do so out of fear—fear that the parents would not believe them, that they might agree with the punishment, or worse, of getting more slaps and stinging words from the parents. Some parents still believe that the rod is the only way of straightening a child out, and they willingly hand the rod to the teacher. For the child it is a lose-lose situation.

The issue of abuse is way more complicated than installing CCTV cameras, writing assurance letters to parents, and holding occasional seminars for the teachers to promote sensitivity. As parents, we cannot be spectators. We must not entrust the schools with absolute power. Yes, schools are an important part of growth but where is the growth in hearing demeaning words or getting slapped by a teacher?

No, I cannot change the system, or sit in the school lobby waiting to meet the principal every day because I fear that someday it could be my son. Neither can I watch my boys sigh in relief each day they successfully avoid the landmines. But that doesn't mean we have to be helpless. The boys and I have a sort of code in place. Some of its tenets are:

- No form of abuse is justifiable. There are no acceptable degrees—an ear tug is as grave as a slap.

- Good touch-bad touch is not just for young kids. Stepping into their teens doesn't make children any less vulnerable.
- Just because they are boys doesn't mean that people can be rough with them. And no, the roughness they face doesn't necessarily equip them to deal with the harsh world later. If anything, it makes them more vulnerable.
- The boys are encouraged to discuss each and every mundane detail of their schoolday. That is how I know which teachers have a crazy violent streak, and which are the nice ones who truly love doing what they do. And the discussion never ends in a moral lecture. Ever.
- I am a teacher, too. Respecting teachers is the norm for them, but they also understand respect doesn't mean absolute power and that teachers can be flawed too. So, while they are respectful, they are also aware of what is unacceptable behaviour, and so far have reported everything they think is worth reporting.
- From the boys' middle-school days, since they had a 'reputation' to protect, I did not just stomp into the school office to discuss any problems that they faced. First, they are encouraged to work out a solution. Then, if the matter is more serious, we discuss possible solutions ranging from migrating out of the country (usually the first idea they come up with) to standing up for what is right. Ultimately, it is the boys' decision to let me in. If I go and discuss something they told me in confidence, I lose their trust. On the other hand, if I convince them through logic that it is the right thing to do, then we all win.

This might not be a foolproof method, but it seems to be working. We keep adding to the code and modifying existing clauses as we go along.

Recently, the same issue cropped up again. A teacher had been hitting students regularly.

'Did you get hit too?' I asked.

'Nope. I guess I was spared because he thinks I am a good student.'

'But he hits other boys badly?'

'Yes. And threatens them a lot. What do you think we should do?'

A voice inside me was saying that since he was in the teacher's good books, we should let it go. But another little voice was telling me to go and report it. I told him exactly what I felt. Children are more equipped to handle complex emotions than we give them credit for.

'So which voice would you listen to?' he asked me.

'What do you think?'

'I think the other voice is right. But what if he finds out it was me and then takes it out on me?'

'Then I don the cape.'

Teenage Romance

In the news: Fifteen-year-old commits suicide over objections to her friendship with a boy.

Elsewhere: A school berates two eighth-grade students who were found in 'objectionable' circumstances, and quietly and swiftly sends them home. Rumours of their expulsion float. The children are conspicuously absent from school.

At home: Ishaan asks me, 'What do you think I should do if a girl has a crush on me?'

Teenage sexuality is real, but sadly remains taboo. We shake our heads at that other kid, and firmly believe that our child is not interested in all that 'nonsense'. The schools are in a hurry to wash their hands of it. The easiest route is usually suspension or, worse, expulsion, with no thought of how this is going to affect the young people involved.

This is our fault, as parents and as a society. We pretend that a teenager is just a grumpy, slouchy, overgrown child. We choose to focus exclusively on academics as the determinant of a child's future value in adult society. We send them to school for an education, not romantic interludes. (We say this huffily, forgetting our own crushes at the same age.) However, everything matters—academics, relationships, crushes, thoughts, feelings—everything.

But things are changing. I see parents asking on social media about how to react to teenage crushes. At least, they are wondering; there are beginnings of dialogue somewhere. But is it enough? Schools need to wake up, as do we.

We might not want teenage romance to exist but it does. We may think that school-time romances are not important, but for the young people involved, they are. So, what do we do? How one approaches it, and what words one uses are personal choices. I have not had to face it so far, but I hope I will deal with it thus:

HOW TO DEAL WITH TEENAGE ROMANCE

👍 Accept the inevitable

Teenage romance is real. Has always been. In the proverbial 'our times', it was less talked about. Now, with social media taking over a big chunk of communication, and the added openness in relationships, it is in our faces. This simply means that there will be crushes, heartbreaks and stolen kisses. Once we have accepted this reality, we can help our children understand what boundaries there ought to be and why.

Communicate

Communication is always a two-way street. Don't limit it to 'What happened at school?' or 'Did you get any homework?'

This does not mean that you interrogate your child, or bore them with sermons. Sentences like 'Who are your friends?' or 'That boy? You better stay away from him!' are pointless and don't serve any purpose.

Communication requires us, among other things, to share details about our lives in order to elicit unguarded responses from our children. If you want your child to talk about her life to you, talk to her about your life and thoughts, and do not be judgemental or preachy about what she tells you.

Be neutral

Don't be too judgemental about the stories your child tells you of his day at school or things his friends said. Some of the things I hear from the boys, well, I am tempted to tell them that it is not completely acceptable. But I resist. When we correct them every step of the way, they stop sharing. Telling a child what good boys or good girls do or not do has never led to epiphanies for the child. It leads to doors being shut and wormholes being blocked off so that you are left feeling your way around in the dark.

For the teens or preteens, their feelings are very real and important. If they have a crush on someone, it is true love. If someone else has a crush on them, they are genuinely confused. Since it is the first time that they are experiencing this kind of attraction or intensity of emotion, listen to what they have to say and help them articulate what they feel. You cannot dismiss it as unimportant or wrong.

Talk about love

Do not make love or attraction a taboo topic, and do not show disrespect for it, even if you are personally cynical about it. It helps if you talk about love in general to your preteen child, encourage your child to share what she feels about it. This goes a long way in arming her with the capability to understand what she is feeling when the time comes.

A while back, Vivaan had described attraction as a funny feeling in the stomach. Now, however, he has gone back to being confused about girls. But we talked about the funny feeling then, and we discuss his confusion now.

Chances are that your teenager already has a fair idea about sex. If she is lucky, she has a sound sex education module at school, or you have mustered up enough courage to talk to her about it. If you haven't, do it now. It is never too late. Pick a good sex education book, sit her down, read with her, and discuss. Acknowledge that she might feel sexual attraction at some point in her life. Teach her to evaluate her feelings. Focus on unprotected sex and its repercussions—physical and emotional, not moral.

Accept differences

Sexual orientation, skin tone, religion, caste—these are all just labels. If you have accustomed your mind to the idea that teenage romance might happen, think further. Expecting the person in question to be of what is to you the acceptable gender, caste or religion is delusional. Your child has made her choice, and as a parent, you need to accept that she has the right to do so.

Being gay is not a disease. And no there is no 'cure'. Yes, it is hard—for your child and for you. Now more than ever, she needs your staunch support. Falling in love with someone from another caste or religion would not lead to the end of the world. Look at your child as a person independent of labels. If you think she is making a mistake, be there to support her if and when she falls. Let her choose. There is a world out there that she needs to fight off. You have to be her ally, her armour.

👍 Help your child deal with peer pressure

Sometimes it is perceived—in the strange, fraught world that is middle school and high school—that 'cool kids' have love interests. And this drives other kids to want to pair off as well. If children are taught to deal with peer pressure, and made to feel comfortable in their skin, things are smoother.

If your child has a partner, peer pressure can often play a role in shaping how the relationship progresses. Discuss with your child how she should only do what she feels comfortable doing, not what is decreed by the peer group.

The boys have described how some kids are ridiculed for not having girlfriends, with the bullies going to the extent of challenging their sexual orientation. We, together, try to figure out what things truly matter.

👍 Distract

A child who is preoccupied with a million things she loves is less likely to fall into the trap of peer pressure or curiosity. The boys learn guitar, read like maniacs, and play at least one sport of their choice. We try to incorporate varied experiences in our lives—from watching superhero movies, to attending book festivals and history walks.

Multiple interests also help children tide over heartbreaks. Where there is love, broken hearts cannot be far behind. Movie dates with your child, and more stuff to take her mind off the trauma, helps her move on.

👍 Be philosophical

Teenage romances are learning grounds for young people to understand complex feelings, to deal with rejection, and to respect each other. Romantic relationships are a major developmental milestone, irrespective of whether the teenagers learn through experience or observation of one's peers. From identity development to changes in self-respect, romantic relationships impact a lot of areas. Ignoring their existence results in turning a blind eye to developmental changes that they might effect.

Resist the urge to cry

Or whack your child. Or lock her up. Or ...

Keep calm. You will survive. It is also helpful to watch *Qayamat Se Qayamat Tak*, *Romeo and Juliet* or *Julie* and remind yourself that that is not how you want things to pan out. Have faith in your child and in your parenting.

As a parent, I want my boys to know that love happens, to know that there are boundaries, and to know I am there, and I will always stand with them. As a parent, I do not want them to confuse morality with the strange feeling in the tummy. Getting attracted to someone doesn't make them immoral. Shunning love in one's growing years does not make one a good human being; good deeds and thoughts do. I want them to learn that difference.

DEALING WITH FRIENDS & FAMILY

Sibling Rivalry

A bloodcurdling scream rang out. Then an ominous silence. I froze. The only sound came from the dog still snoring at my footstep.

In my mind, I was chanting, 'God, please spare me this once. Just this once.' But, alas, it was not to be.

A few seconds after the scream, the two boys stormed into my room.

'He dog-eared my book!'

'You said there is no mine-thine in this house as far as books are concerned!'

'Dog-eared! How could you?' A short scuffle followed.

The dog stirred, and stopped snoring.

The boys, not satisfied by my silence, took the scuffle outside. After a muffled argument, a pair of feet stomped in. 'I hate him! I wish he was not my brother.'

For a few seconds my blood boils, my jaw clenches, and my head bursts with a million words I want to hurl at them. Then, I get back to reading, writing, or pretending to work at something more important. And he slinks away, still grumbling.

Barely half an hour later, I congratulate myself for the restraint shown, since the two of them are happily engrossed in training the five dogs to sit in a line.

But each day doesn't end like this. There are days when I shed secret tears of exhaustion from playing the peacemaker. I am learning to step back, to reinvent strategies and, most importantly, to stay calm.

There are certain ground rules that work for me most of the time, keeping the parental sanity levels within permissible limits.

RULES FOR HANDLING SIBLING RIVALRY

Refuse to be the referee

Most fights end with the boys running to me for a resolution. Being a referee also means taking sides. Unless the guilty party is fairly apparent, I refuse to get involved.

This doesn't mean that I stay silent. Once you are sure that it is not a bully-victim situation (which it isn't as far as my household is concerned), hold both of them responsible, and dish out an equal 'sentence' to both. So whenever these two come to me fighting, they both lose out on something they like—staying up late, watching television, or anything else that would get them to ponder the wisdom in escalating the fight.

Acknowledge emotions

Anger and jealousy are as much a part of the emotional spectrum as love. It is futile to ignore them, and worse to counter them with guilt. If a child is feeling a twang of jealousy, acknowledge it. If one of them is angry with the other for taking his stuff, breaking something, or simply stepping into his room, accept the anger. The idea is to help them learn to deal with these emotions and not make them feel small by labelling such emotions as blasphemous.

Do not compare

'Your brother eats everything, you do not.' 'Learn something from your sister, she works so hard.' 'Why can't you be like your brother?' Statements like these are guaranteed to make siblings each other's sworn enemies. It gets difficult sometimes, but watch what you say or imply. Comparison breeds contempt. Celebrate their differences.

The angry hour

Each day, when they fight, set aside half an hour for anger. During this time, they are supposed to sit and argue. Half an hour of forced argument is enough to motivate the boys to stay away from fights.

Initially when I'd sense an argument coming, I'd remind them of where they were heading. They ended up sitting around the table a few times, at a loss for words after a five-minute argument followed by twenty-five minutes of fidgety silence or uncontrollable giggles. And that is all it took for peace to prevail for some time.

The cooperation jar

This is a true gem! Label a clear glass jar with their names, and set ground rules. Every time they indulge in cooperative play they get two bonus coins; each day without a fight translates into one bonus coin, and each act of kindness towards each other results in a whopping three. On the flip side, each fight leads to two coins being taken out. The idea is for them to spend their loot together once the jar is filled to the brim. So far, it is working.

👍 Me time

Set aside some time each day for one-on-one conversation. At that time, the other child is not to be allowed in the room. Listen to them. Most problems get diffused, if they know that they are getting their share of attention. Plan some outings that involve only one of them.

That serves two purposes—first, they get their share of undivided attention, and second, they learn to respect that not every moment will be identical for both of them. The tricky part is to make sure that both get their share of fun and neither feels left out.

👍 Deep breaths

Children often mirror what they see. So if you are stressed most of the time, getting angry a lot, and yelling at them at the first inkling of a fight, chances are they will take to bickering among themselves with a greater fervour.

This is tough. I have to really grit my teeth at times to prevent myself from bursting with anger. But the fact remains that the days I stick to staying calm, things calm down quicker than the days I get mad. To manage your child's anger spells, you have to learn to manage yours first.

👍 The no-tolerance zone

Some things have to be absolutely unacceptable. I have made a short 'thou shalt not' list of things that shall awaken the wrath of the gods. It includes fistfights, breaking each other's stuff, name-calling and yelling at each other. The consequences range from detention to taking away the most favoured toy or a privilege for a week.

These measures have helped. Peace does not prevail at all times, but things are definitely better than before. After a day of mostly restrained, and few unrestrained fights, the boys grudgingly go to sleep in the same room, despite having their own independent ones. When I go to check on them, they are blissfully asleep, sometimes holding each other's hands.

Friendship Across Genders

Ask any kid, and chances are they'd be horrified at the prospect of being friends with the opposite sex. Both boys and girls have pretty strong opinions about each other, which range from being negative to outright hostile.

Mixed-gender friendships change with age. Toddlers are often found playing with each other irrespective of gender. By the age of four, children understand their gender and its stability. By seven years, they also know that changing appearances, clothes, or hair length doesn't make them a boy or a girl. Gender identity, which now begins to strengthen, is their first step towards formation of a social identity outside the family. This is further strengthened by associating with members of the same sex to the complete exclusion of the other.

This is also the time when culturally determined gender roles start to creep in. Statements like 'girls are sensitive' or 'boys do not cry' start getting absorbed. The two genders start feeling fierce prejudices towards each other, and friendships are formed with members of the same sex. So basically, a boy learns that he is a boy and what makes him that, mixes exclusively with other boys, and further strengthens his gender identity by degrading the opposite sex. Sad, but true.

This goes on until adolescence when, thanks to a cocktail of hormones coupled with other factors, most kids find themselves getting attracted to the opposite sex. If kids grow up seeing stereotypical images of a girl being submissive and a boy being aggressive, it often sets the tone for future relationships.[6]

In today's world—where gender boundaries are blurring in the professional world at least, and where there is a sharp rise in gender-related bias—there is an urgent need to teach children about friendship and its relative independence from gender.

HOW CROSS-GENDER FRIENDSHIPS HELP DEVELOP LIFE SKILLS

- The only way attitudes towards the members of the opposite sex changes is through interaction. Mixed-gender friendships teach both the boys and the girls to respect each other and accept them as individuals rather than just as a 'boy or a 'girl'.
- Children find themselves in a fix if they are required to interact with members of the opposite sex. I remember a dance class back in school—our teacher pulled her hair out trying to get us to lock arms without giggling or jeering. Being friends, regardless of gender, increases social competence.
- Playing, spending time with, and generally being friends with the opposite gender also teaches boundaries and

lays a foundation for handling future relationships, including marriage.

- And, ultimately, a well-adjusted work life. When you grow up being friends with the opposite sex, chances are that you would respect someone for the work they do regardless of their gender. When my son comes home and appreciates his friend for her exceptional mathematical prowess, I swell with pride since in him I see an adult who wouldn't degrade his female co-workers for being women.

Although it is an uphill task, considering that friendships happen outside the home and are largely affected by the external world, as parents, we can help our children make the right choices and fight the tide.

HOW TO ENCOURAGE MIXED-GENDER FRIENDSHIPS

👍 Bust gender stereotypes

Since cross-gender friendships are largely affected by prejudice against the opposite gender, try to lessen stereotyping. A boy playing with a doll or a girl exploring Lego trucks is perfectly fine.

👍 Encourage kids to express their feelings

Statements like 'boys are wild' and 'girls are sweet' should be forbidden. If a girl is angry, let her express her rage and if a boy is hurt, it is okay for him to shed a tear. Acknowledge a wide range of emotions irrespective of gender.

👍 Encourage mixed-gender activities

A lot of times, schools as well as parents hint at the suitability of certain activities for a specific gender. Girls are made to join cooking classes and you rarely see boys playing sports like throwball. Encourage children to experiment and ask the school to form mixed-gender teams.

👍 Do not make a big deal out of mixed-gender interactions

Parents are sometimes phobic at the prospect of children mingling with the opposite sex. If the child is discussing a classmate, be interested regardless of the gender of the kid being talked about. Do not appear overly interested when the child is discussing someone of the opposite sex.

👍 Birds and bees help

Lack of knowledge increases the distance between the two genders. If they know the differences, they are also likely to understand their insignificance in determining a person.

👍 Treat equally

Often, I see parents handling boys and girls differently. When you meet your son's female classmate, be as casual as you'd be with the boys and vice versa. You don't have to soften your tone or be gentler than you normally are—girls aren't made of porcelain and neither are boys made of coarse stone. The fewer differences they perceive, the better it is.

👍 Teach them to deal with teasing

When Vivaan was nine, he came home seething with anger. His classmates had teased him for talking to his female friend and called them 'girlfriend-boyfriend'. So, we talked about how teasing is a milder form of bullying. Anything out of the ordinary becomes a target. We can't sit the world down and change it, but we can build a shield around ourselves and not be affected. This is what worked for us when he got teased:

- Teach your child to believe in his own self rather than forcing himself into a traditional gender role.
- Teach him to evaluate the importance of his friends, males as well as females.
- Ask him to question what is more important, his friend, or the silly teasing.
- Discuss with (and not tell) the child how it is fine to be different, and unacceptable to end friendships out of fear of jibes from other kids.
- Never look upset when the child comes home and tells you about being teased. If you are upset, he will not tell you the next time.
- Be compassionate, ask questions, give honest answers, and never get over-protective. When your child questions you about it, tell him that he might get teased but that you are confident that he can handle it. Practice role-playing to model appropriate responses.

These are some things that all of us can start with. The long-term effects of sex segregation are still a matter of research; however, it is very clear that mixed-gender peer interactions benefit a child's holistic growth.

Talking about Death and Grief

It all began with Jenny. The doctor tut-tutted as he took a closer look at the ultrasound machine's screen. It all looked like shades of black and grey to me but he shook his head gravely, while a pair of trusting eyes stared back at me from the table.

The journey back home was spent contemplating how to break it to the children. In fact, how do you break it to anyone? 'I am sorry but your pet is dying.' 'We have to let her go.' What are the right words? What is the right tone? How much information is too much?

We came back and made Jenny comfortable in her room. Her perked-up ears and faintly wagging stub of a tail gave no sign that the cancer had spread to all her vital organs and that the tumour could burst any time. All we could do was make her comfortable.

The boys' questions started pouring in. I decided to play it straight. When the story of their birth never involved storks or any such nonsense, the story of losing their pet should be honest too. They heard it all—about her condition, the reports, the prognosis and the way forward.

After a short silence, Vivaan quietly concluded, 'I read somewhere that Mother Teresa had once said that everyone deserves a beautiful death. I think we should just love Jenny a lot.'

I had been expecting tears, sobs and fits of anger. But here they were, two boys stronger than me at the prospect of losing a friend they had had for most of their lives.

We never shirk from discussing anything, no matter how uncertain or ominous it is. Death has been discussed extensively and both the boys have their own takes about the journey thereafter. When they lost their great-grandpa, I sat them down, and amidst tears and hugs gave them the facts—no turning into angels or going away somewhere, just plain facts. Once the facts were absorbed, we moved on to a more philosophical discussion.

When a loved pet dies, statements like 'god took her away', 'he was put to sleep' or 'he is in heaven now' confuse the children if made without any discussion. I feel that an honest, age-appropriate discussion is the best way to prepare the little ones. Talking about illness and the helplessness of watching loved ones fade does more good than harm. As a parent, I am not supposed to have all the answers. It is okay to tell them what I think happens after death, which might be entirely different from what they feel. It is okay to let them know that I am grieving too and that it is perfectly acceptable for them to feel sad.

I know that their reaction does not mean they are fine with it. A few days later, while playing with his Megatron action figure, Vivaan asked, 'Mum, do you miss Richie?'

Richie was my dog whom I had lost roughly eighteen years earlier.

'Not anymore.'

'So, it doesn't hurt?'

'Not for long.'

'Hmm.' Megatron had attacked Bumblebee, so the questions were lost in the battle for now.

When the time comes, there are going to be tears and hugs. There are going to be lots of questions—maybe some very morbid ones involving the prospect of losing people they love. The approach will remain the same: honest, patient answers. Every child is different and needs to be helped differently.

Two years later, it was my grandmother. 'I miss her,' I whispered as I lay on the sliver of space on the bed.

Vivaan finally said, 'Will you be all right? I still miss Jenny sometimes. Terribly. I hate death.' Soon, tears, mixed with whispered conversation about fears associated with dying, flowed freely. The older one mostly hugged me.

As parents, the most dreaded talk, right after sex, is talking about losing someone dear to us. Losing a pet, hearing about someone else dying or losing a family member—all of these are extremely distressing, especially to children, and hence we try everything to protect them from the truth. Mostly, we lie. The pet usually runs off or goes to visit someone, depending on the age of the child being lied to. The difficulties we face in explaining death to our children are understandable. We can explain most things in easy terms, but to explain something that we ourselves do not fully understand is undoubtedly a challenge.

HOW TO TALK TO KIDS ABOUT DEATH

👍 Be honest

We often define dying as 'going away' to children. Avoid saying a person has 'gone away', was 'lost' or 'has 'passed away'. Due to a fairly literal understanding of language, this leads to confusion and insecurity.

Do not shy away from using the D-word. For example, when someone dies, they stop eating, breathing, feeling our touch, and eventually we cannot see them any more. As a rough marker, a child of five begins to understand the permanence of death. After that, depending on the age, it can be dealt with from increasingly complex perspectives as the child grows older. If there is something we do not know the answer to, it is best to say so, rather than serve up lies.

👍 Let death be a part of conversation

Books are great for starting such conversations. A character dying can be a good, emotionally distant place to start the discussion. If a child overhears a piece of news about someone dying, don't change the channel, talk and listen instead.

There are many age-appropriate books and movies that can be used to initiate a conversation about death. My favourite movie out of these is *The Lion King*.

Apart from *The Lion King*, and the movie versions of some of the books listed below, some of the other movies I would recommend are:

Up
Finding Nemo
The Land Before Time
Marley & Me
Hachi: A Dog's Tale

For Your Bookshelf

Goodbye Mog by Judith Kerr
The Flat Rabbit by Bardur Oskarsson
The Scar by Charlotte Moundlic
Duck, Death and the Tulip by Wolf Erlbruch
Cry, Heart, but Never Break by Glenn Ringtved
The Elephant in the Room: A Children's Book for Grief and Loss by Amanda Edwards, Leslie Ponciano, Julia Horwitz
Missing Mommy: A Book about Bereavement by Rebecca Cobb
Sad Book by Michael Rosen
Counting by 7s by Holly Goldberg Sloan
A Monster Calls by Patrick Ness
Bridge to Terabithia by Katherine Paterson
The *Harry Potter* series by J.K. Rowling

👍 It is okay to display your emotions

We sometimes try to clam up in front of children. Hiding our emotions doesn't help them deal with their own. We are giving them the message that it is not okay to hurt. On the contrary, if the child sees you being disturbed, he is more likely to accept the pain, and share his grief with you. Crying is natural reaction to pain. And it is okay for a child to learn that.

👍 Never hide information

When my grandfather was hospitalised, I didn't tell the boys. When he passed away, we went for the funeral, again without telling them. In the evening when I came back, they were a bundle of nerves. When I finally told them, they felt betrayed. They had sensed that something was wrong since I had been gone for a long time, and the ambiguity of the situation had scared the wits out of them. It took a lot of hugs and apologies to calm them down. That day I vowed to never hide information from them, no matter how grave it was. So when my grandma was in the hospital, they knew. When her condition deteriorated, they shared my pain. And when she passed away, I told them upfront.

👍 Be patient

Each child grieves differently. He could seem indifferent to a grandparent's passing but have a complete meltdown at losing a goldfish. There are no prescribed reactions. They are still learning theirs. When the boys went for Jenny's burial, there were tears. But tears do not ensure catharsis. So we talked about her. The boys drew her, and wrote about her. All this helps. There might be times when the child brings up a pet's passing, months later. Do not dismiss it. Stop and listen. After a good two years, when I whispered that I miss my Nani, the younger one's memory of his experience with death in the form of Jenny's departure came back. And we talked again.

👍 If needed, seek help

Sometimes, no matter what we do, the child is not able to fully cope with grief. This can in turn lead to behavioural changes. For a long time after Jenny's death, the younger one was irritable, and would refuse to talk about it. So we painted a rock with Jenny on it, and downloaded some excellent books that he could write in. The rock is still in his room, and writing in the grief book helped him come to terms with it. At times, however, whatever parents may do isn't enough and professional help is needed. In such situations, a counsellor should be approached.

👍 Refresh memories

The ultimate step in dealing with pain is talking about happy memories. Losing someone is scary and painful, but this loss does not have to snatch the joyful moments you spent with that person. And these very smiles help us carry on through painful times. So, sometimes when we are lazing around, I tell them about their 'big Nani'. I relate stories to them. Sometimes, the conversation trails off into a few tears, and at others, we end up smiling. These are all natural steps towards healing.

👍 Let them find their way

The other day, I saw the younger one sneak up to Jenny's grave and quickly leave a piece of mithai there. He ran back in, making sure no one saw him. We developed it into a ritual. So, every time other dogs get a treat, her share is left at her grave. This helps him deal with it without the added stress of hiding. Some children prefer to talk about it. While some find their own ways like my younger one. Irrespective of the path to healing they take, it is important that we are with them all the way.

It is tough. But I do not lie anymore. If I go to a prayer meeting, I tell them about it and try to answer whatever they want to know. I let them help me through grief and I try to help them in theirs. We accept tears; they do not distress us anymore. It is okay if my child cries. I cannot protect them from pain, but I can surely cushion the fall, and help in healing the wound. Death will painfully remain a part of our lives. It will keep scarring our soul, and we accept that. Running from this reality makes us way more out of breath than when we get punched in the gut by grief. So we do not run anymore. We stop, clasp our hands tight, and weather the storm.

Taking On Bullying

Early 1970s: A bride receives an unexpected letter. It is from a friend whom, back in college, everyone had called 'flat-chested', 'a boy' and more because she was 'too lean to be a girl'. The bride had also laughed, and never tried to stop anyone. The letter told her that. And it said how much she had valued her as a friend, but how deeply she was hurt since she never stood up for her. The letter still haunts her.

Late 1980s: A girl is 'playfully' taunted for having huge manly hands, and made to feel like an outcast—mostly by other girls. She still tries to hide her hands in the folds of her garments, though she is nearing forty.

2013: 'Oh ho! You know how it is! They are stepping into their teens. They tend to get a bit violent sometimes.' The teacher had been approached by the parent of a preteen. The boy had been severely beaten up by two boys for tattling on them.

Bullying is not taken seriously enough in India. People often dismiss it as 'toughening', 'hormones' or 'learning'.

And we reinforce it by belittling or ignoring it, or worse, lashing out at the child who is going through it all: 'Be tough! It is all a part of growing up!'

Being called names or being beaten up is definitely not a part of any delusional developmental milestone; it is just one thing—bullying. And it is on the rise.

MYTHS ABOUT BULLYING

Calling someone chubby, dark or 'chashmish' is not bullying

'Children do it all the time.' Just because children do it all the time doesn't give it legitimacy. Name-calling or any other form of verbal abuse is to be taken seriously. As adults, we should know the destructive power of words.

A slap shouldn't be taken seriously

Yes, children fight, slap and kick, and then one day the fight gets nasty. If the child is lucky enough to escape, he has learnt a faulty lesson: That it is okay to be oppressed and that a good way of dealing with conflict or insecurity is beating the other person to pulp. And if he isn't lucky, then he gets to be a statistic.

Teachers never bully or aid bullying

At one school PTM, I was told that one of my boys asked too many questions and that this was not good. 'Other kids make fun of him and ridicule him. You know how important it is for them to fit in.'

I sat blinking for a while and then I exploded. We have all heard of teachers ridiculing children, in the name of humour. What the teachers do not realise is that their statements are reinforced even more vindictively by other students.

Girls do not bully

Girls are as capable of bullying as boys and get as nasty.

Bullying is another name for a fight and it is normal for kids to fight

Wrong again. The child being bullied does not choose to fight, and is frequently unable to defend himself.

Bullying is another name for kids being silly

Kids being silly—but with malicious intent and a victim. From behavioural problems, academic disturbance, depression and even suicide, the consequences of bullying have been widely observed and researched.

Bullying toughens kids up

Do you ask your doctor to inject typhoid-causing bacteria into your system so that you can toughen up your digestion? Bullying weakens the child. In no way does it help him become tough. For that, there is love, support and the child's strength of character.

My child would have told me

Statistics show that only one in three bullied kids open up to an adult. The older the victim is, the more averse he is to telling a parent. Kids fear they won't be taken seriously, or that their parents might create a scene at school, thus making the victim an even bigger subject of ridicule.

Bullying is confined to school

Bullying can take place in the classroom, the playground, the neighbourhood park, the school bus, and cyberspace. Bullies are found everywhere, and they find victims everywhere.

👎 My child needs to fight the bully

If your child fights back in the same way he was treated, then he is doing exactly what he had been a victim of. Bullying needs to be dealt with more comprehensively, and retaliation does not solve anything.

👎 Bullying happens in senior school

Bullying happens at all ages. Studies show that it is most rampant in middle school. Grades VI to VIII report the highest number of bullying cases.

What, then, constitutes bullying? Is it just hitting? Or does it include public name-calling? What about secret messages being passed around the class? How do we help children spot bullies, and know if they are being targetd?

Well, in short, a bully is a person who repeatedly hurts a child, whether emotionally or physically. A bully would deliberately make the child feel uncomfortable, unwanted or inferior in some way. She may spread nasty rumours about the victim (offline, online or both), call the victim nasty names, and send threatening or abusive messages.

Bullying is rampant and can happen to anybody. So, how do you protect your child?

HOW SHOULD PARENTS DEAL WITH BULLYING?

👍 Communicate

Encourage your child to tell you about her day in detail. Don't stop at listening, but ask questions and be interested. Get excited at the extra run she took. If you seem disinterested in day-to-day conversations, you cannot expect her to come to you when something serious happens.

👍 Involve the school

Report any incidents that trouble you or your child to the school. Do not let the school play it down or make you feel as if you are a paranoid parent. It is your right to be heard. Dealing with bullying has to be a collaborative effort.

Children are sometimes not aware of what comprises bullying, when the joke stops being funny, and when they overstep boundaries. The school needs to teach the kids, but so do parents. We can't just shake our heads at the school's lack of involvement and turn away from our responsibility.

👍 Recognise the signs

My child is as capable of being a bully as he is of being bullied. Each child needs to be made aware of the consequences. Never assume that your angel-faced baby is not capable of hurting even a fly—he can accomplish much more.

If you see unexplained injuries, sleep or eating disturbances, torn/damaged school supplies, dropping grades—raise a red flag. Your child might be a victim.

On the other hand, if the child is being increasingly aggressive, worrying excessively about his social position in the class, or getting overly competitive, you might want to make sure he isn't bullying anyone. If your child suddenly has lots of unexplained new possessions—toys, stationery, money—that is also reason to look closer.

And then, there is the in-between stage, where the child may not be aware of the implications of certain behaviours, which might be dangerously close to bullying.

I found the boys giggling as Vivaan narrated how an obese classmate had been nicknamed Jumbo.

'That amounts to bullying,' I butted in.

Both of them said in unison, 'No, it doesn't.'

'And besides, Ma, he himself laughs it off.'

I sat them down and explained. Children laugh off the nicknames they are given to avoid further victimisation or isolation. That doesn't mean they like the joke.

Nurture your child's self-confidence

A child who feels good about himself and has high self-esteem is less likely to be affected by bullying. If I constantly tell my child that he is a failure or lacking in some way, I am lowering his self-esteem with every negative word. That obviously doesn't imply that we should create an exaggerated self image—we should stick to positive criticism and praise when due.

Encouraging a child to find something that interests him, and which he is good at helps him become more confident and less susceptible to being victimised.

Don't focus on appearance

The world is sadly very appearance-driven, and it is very common for bullies to target their victims over something to do with how they look. Calling a child short, fat or strange-looking can, over time, hurt him badly.

Most parents love to dress their toddlers up, but when the same children are in their teens and are bothered about their looks or attire, we blame it on hormones. Emphasise (and genuinely believe) that appearance is not important, but also be supportive of your child's concerns about appearance. Teach your child to dress well, but not fuss over the brand of their glasses or shoes. A child who is overly sensitive about his looks is immediately more vulnerable.

Never blame the victim

'What did you do to annoy that child?' 'You must have done something that made them mad enough to hit you.' Never make these statements to a child who has come to confide in you. It must've taken him immense courage to walk up to you and tell you about what happened. This is not the time to tell him where he went wrong, or what he should have done. This is the time to let him know that you are taking it very seriously, and that bullying is strictly unacceptable. Let him know that you are with him.

Urge your child to help victims of bullying

An unconcerned bystander aids the bully. This doesn't imply that you have to teach your child to jump into the fray every time. Encourage him to be sympathetic to the victim. Often, what a child being bullied needs most is friends who stand by him and give him the courage to do what he cannot do—report the bully to a teacher or a parent.

Cyberbullying is a reality

If you read the news, you will know that there are many kids who are victims of cyberbullying.

Control your child's access to the internet. Be vigilant and install parental checks and filters. Make sure your child is comfortable coming to you to talk, without fearing your yelling at him above the amount of time he spends online.

If needed, get professional help

Sometimes kids need help in dealing with the pain, shame and agony of having faced a bully, and going through hell at school. Be vigilant for signs of your child being bullied.

If there are noticeable behavioural changes, or persistent reluctance to go to school even after the incidents of bullying have been reported, get help.

If you think your child is the victim of bullying, do not freak out. Keep calm and work out with your child how he wishes to deal with the situation. You can suggest the following tips to the child.

HOW SHOULD THE VICTIM DEAL WITH THE BULLY?

Tell the bully to stop

The child should calmly but firmly tell the bully to stop. He should reinforce it by holding up his hand. Sometimes a firm protest will discourage the bully. If humour is your child's thing, he could try using humour.

Walk away

The child should get away from the situation, possibly to a crowded area, and seek help from an adult.

Don't panic

The child should not show that he is affected. The bully looks for signs that the victim is upset because that gives him the satisfaction of having some power over the victim.

Seek help

The child should talk to a teacher, a friend or a parent, and make them listen. He should be as calm as possible while reporting the incident so that he is taken seriously.

Stick with other kids

Two or three kids are tougher to pick on when they are together. Ask your child to get his friends to band together to speak out about the bully, or just for safety.

Don't carry unnecessary stuff to school

Gadgets, money and fancy stuff often attracts bullies. Ask your child to not carry things he does not need to school.

As parents, we have to ensure that childhood is as joyful as it can be for our children. Bullying ruins lives—it doesn't matter if the victim is a preschooler or an eleventh-grader. No one deserves to be degraded, humiliated or made to feel weak or unworthy. It is time that we took bullying seriously in all its forms, and collaborated to address this issue. It is time we stood by our child's side.

Body Shaming

Humiliating someone by making mocking or critical comments about their body shape or size is a problem, that seems to increase with every passing year. It starts as early as junior school, with nicknames like Jumbo and Chashmish, and gets meaner and more vicious as children grow up. By teenage, it is a problem that is endemic.

Because it seems to be so superficial, children may feel troubled articulating it to parents, or even to themselves. One's body is what it is, and while adults also struggle with it, children are frequently devastated by it.

The first and most important rule is that as a parent, you have to support your child. Never criticise your child's appearance.

As with anything to do with appearance, girls have it harder. But because people largely associate body shaming with women, there is more visible support for girls and even public condemnation of fairness creams and size-zero figures. We are quick to condemn boys who body-shame girls.

But while it is important to provide girls with as much support as possible to combat and resist body shaming, it is wrong to assume that it is only girls who are shamed for having certain 'undesirable' body characteristics. We assume that boys do not care about appearance, and that there is no problem to be resolved.

Any time I had mentioned appearance-related issues to the boys, they had just rolled their eyes at me. So, I assumed that this was not an issue for boys—yes, I make wrong assumptions all the time.

All that changed last year when, during a session on bullying, the participating children got talking. A girl related how she was teased because she was dark. A boy grinned and added, 'I am teased because I am too fair!' And that was the opening of Pandora's box. One by one, the boys admitted to getting teased about their weight (or lack of it), fairness (or lack of it), body hair (or lack of it), height (or lack of it) and so on.

Ishaan later told me, 'If they can't really make fun of anything else, they comment on the size of the penis.' He added quickly, 'It hasn't happened to me yet but I know of kids who have been jeered at.'

I was very curious. 'How do they measure it?'

He shrugged and said, 'I don't know. It is just a thing they joke about.'

It is not just girls but also boys who feel that they must live up to unrealistic standards of beauty. Ishaan's friend sent him a photo of his torso, with the caption: 'See! Six-pack abs!' There isn't a single muscle visible unless one mistook the ribs for muscles. But the boy clearly wanted them desperately enough to wish them into being.

As parents, we may be ignoring that our children are being body-shamed, which we turn a blind eye to in the name of manning up. How do you ensure that your child is neither a victim nor a perpetrator?

HOW DO WE FIGHT BODY SHAMING?

Start early

Remember the time your little toddler pretended to be the hero from some movie and flexed his nonexistent muscles? And everyone went 'awww' or patted him for possessing such strong arms? That is where it starts.

Resist praising your child for masculine or feminine stereotypes. Or calling your child too fat or too skinny. If you want your child to not care about appearance, then your praise and criticism must not be related to their looks.

Emphasise good health

Good health should never be confused with beautiful bodies. Encourage your child to play, not because she needs to build muscles but because that is the path to good health. Sports should be a part of the routine—for girls as well as boys.

If your child is not too fond of sports, find a physical activity she likes—dancing, swimming, skating, cycling. It is also important that children are encouraged to have a healthy diet from an early age.

Discuss real vs imaginary

Reality is distorted in the male and female bodies in movies, ads, video games and superhero graphic novels. Boys wanting six-pack abs are as common as girls aspiring to size-zero figures. We can't block out these movies or advertisements but we can educate our kids about 'real' bodies and the so-called 'ideal' bodies propagated in some forms of media.

👍 Be happy with your body

Children learn by observation. If your child sees you obsess about your appearance—the love handles, the paunch, the bald spot—she gathers that physical attributes are very important.

If we want our children to grow up respecting others for what they are and not how they look, and loving themselves, we need to truly believe in it ourselves. If you tell your child that appearances are not important, and in the next hour comment that 'Mrs Chatterjee is so fat it is disgusting!', then you are sending confusing messages to her.

Learn to be comfortable with your own body before you preach to your child to be comfortable with hers. Otherwise, your sermons will not ring true.

👍 Encourage sharing of emotions

If your child is able to freely share her anxieties, what the kids at school laughed about or what angered them, a lot of the battle is won.

Sadly, our culture encourages boys to stay quiet. But as parents, we need to resist this stereotyping. They need to know that they are humans first, children second and boys much later. If your son cries, wrap him in a warm hug instead of saying, 'Boys don't cry.' And the best way to get them to share is to share with them first.

👍 Discuss responses

Children often do not know how to react in body-shaming situations. They feel too embarrassed to retort or protest. If you feel your child is vulnerable, it might help to discuss possible responses. Saying something like 'no, you are not dark' reiterates the original taunt. However, replacing it with 'colours don't matter' or 'we are much more than the colour of our skin' makes a difference.

If your child sees you reply calmly or walk away in a poised manner in situations where someone shames you or someone else is shamed in your presence, it will act as a powerful example for her to emulate.

Both Barbie and Superman project unrealistic body images, detrimental to all children. We need to counteract this by giving our kids better role models, and by acknowledging the stupidity of a world obsessed with appearances.

Raising Responsible Boys

'Girls can't fight,' they said.

So, I defeated both of them in a Nerf gun face-off. And I confiscated their guns.

'You were saying?' I asked in a distinctly superior tone as they pleaded for their guns.

'Girls can not only fight, but can also kick our sorry backsides at it,' mumbled Vivaan.

'Huh? Did you say something?'

A sound apology later, we settled for goodnight hugs.

Yes, an apology—for making a generic gender statement. Yes, it was a game, and yes, it was said in jest, but that is exactly how it all starts. 'Girls whine', 'girls can't fight', 'girls do not play cricket', 'girls love to cook'. These are not random harmless statements. They lay the foundation for the dark wall that defines gender boundaries.

Minimising sexism is one of the most daunting tasks that we, as parents, face today. Sexism is now a deeply ingrained part of society—from seemingly harmless stereotyping to abominable acts of sexual violence. We shield our children from news pertaining to rape and other sexual attacks. But as parents, the onus is on us to raise a generation of braver and more respectful men than before, and of stronger, more independent women.

In December 2012, there was a heinous case of a young woman being raped in the middle of Delhi, who subsequently died. I was hiding newspapers, hurrying to switch channels, and having hushed conversations—all in a bid to protect the boys from news of gruesome acts of violation. But one cannot protect beyond a point. Eight-year-old Vivaan asked me: 'What is rape?' I explained as simply as I could, and tried to answer every query they had.

But am I doing enough? Are we—as mothers of sons—doing enough? When people casually tell me, 'What do you have to worry, you have sons!' I flinch. As the mother of sons, I feel I have a special responsibility to bring up boys who are respectful of women and treat them as true equals.

THE DELUSIONS OF MOTHERS OF SONS

My boy can never do such a thing

Any boy, irrespective of financial, or educational background can be tempted to misbehave with girls, belittle them or harass them. So, the sooner you lose that illusion about innocence, the better. The only way to be sure is to educate and sensitise your son much as you can.

Dolls for girls, trucks for boys

If your son plays with dolls, he won't grow up to be a sissy, any more than a girl who plays with Nerf guns will grow a moustache. There is no connection between acceptable masculine behaviour and choice of toys. There is, however, a definite connection between varied, healthy choices and a wholesome personality growth. Vivaan loves to cuddle up with his stuffed raccoon, and sissy wouldn't be the word anyone would use for him!

My son is like a TV hero

In many TV shows and movies (there are, of course, exceptions), the girl forever needs rescuing, boys tease girls but are loved by them, and women are shown as bejewelled, manipulative cooks. Keep a check on the media your child is consuming and have gender-related reality checks every once in a while.

Boys will be boys!

Stop saying 'you know how boys are!' or justifying rude or irresponsible behaviour. A dash of testosterone should not translate into aggression and result in violence. Aggression of any form is not acceptable, period.

He doesn't behave like that

If you are shouting at the maid, you are teaching your son that it is okay to be rude to less privileged women. It is fine to argue with girls in his school, but he cannot talk to them any differently from boys he has disagreements with. And he cannot use sexist language. Irrespective of gender, fights are simply not permitted.

Don't cry like a girl!

The mechanism for crying is fairly similar, regardless of gender! Saying that a boy is crying like a girl tops the list of silliest but also most destructive things ever said. You are telling your son that men do not cry, so whatever is bothering him needs to be ignored, not resolved. And you are telling him that crying is an inferior thing to do, that girls cry and are, therefore, inferior.

If your son is crying over a dead sparrow, an emaciated beggar, or the pet he lost last week—don't shuffle uncomfortably. Give him a hug, and appreciate his sensitivity.

Encouraging boys to talk about feelings and discussing dilemmas will make them stronger men, not weaker. And they will generally be more sorted, and not see themselves as stronger than, or very different from, women.

My son doesn't need to know about sexism

If you do not teach your son about sexism, how will he learn what is unacceptable behaviour? It takes a lot of conversations and reinforcements to overcome the casual sexism of schools, and the world around. Be honest, and they will listen.

Aww, he is still a baby!

Even when your son is fifty, he will still be your baby. But that does not mean that he will still be a baby to the rest of the world. It is up to you to be aware of the fact that he is growing up and teach him about personal space and grown-up behaviour, and help him to adapt to the changed expectations from him as he grows up.

My son will never date

He will, so you should help him understand boundaries that he needs to respect in a relationship. Teenage romance lays the foundation for how your son treats his partners—whether girlfriends or boyfriends—in future relationships. You need to be the mother he can discuss his relationships with, but also the mother who serves as a constant reminder that he needs to treat his partners with respect.

Male role models are important, so encourage your partner to put away the laptop, newspaper or phone. It is important for your son to see that his father respects women and takes an equal part in domestic and parenting responsibilities. If your partner makes statements that reinforce gender biases, now is the time to make him stop.

As the mother of two boys, I feel I have an additional responsibility. I try to undo all that they learn when they step out. I try to get them to see that gender equality doesn't imply crossing boundaries. I try to get them to try varied books, and activities that are callously labelled girly. I try to teach them to question, seek answers, and constantly evolve.

Yes, I am a mother of two boys, and no my fears are no lesser than yours.

The Other Side of the Coin

'I can't not do anything, anymore,' a choked-up Ishaan blurted out over the phone.

'What? What happened?'

'She hit me again, the bully I told you about. And this time I hit her back.'

Alarm bells went off in my head as he related the story. She had been bullying him for some time now, and he had been ignoring it. Ishaan would never hit back on principle, and she is a girl.

Ishaan has learnt to respect girls as equals and peers. But I had never foreseen a situation where he would be confronted with a girl who was bullying him. His teachers failed to see that he was being bullied and ended up lecturing him instead.

And the double whammy was this: The bully was trying to take advantage of her gender. She threatened to complain to the coordinator. And the boys were intimidated because they know a complaint to the coordinator by a girl against a boy wouldn't end well.

As a feminist, I am confused. I have always championed equal rights and believed girls and boys are equal. I believe there needs to be some positive discrimination for women to undo centuries of repression. But I also naively believed that girls and women would use this opportunity responsibly, and not abuse it.

Today, I stand on shaky grounds. When my son couldn't understand why he was being scolded at school for standing up to a bully, all I could do was express my helplessness. 'I hear you, but getting into a fight with a girl is not a good idea. I will always stand with you, but promise me you'll refrain from getting into a fight with her.'

As I drove home, I mulled over my words. I have always stood up for what I believed was right. I have always encouraged my sons to do what they believe is right. But now, instead of confronting the bully, which is what I had told them all their lives to do, I was asking Ishaan to back down in fear.

As parents, we face the daunting task of instilling a deep sense of self-worth in our sons and daughters but never at the cost of anyone else's self-respect. We need to teach them to accept equality as the basis of their lives, and to respect each other as human beings, regardless of gender. Enforcing equality is much more difficult—true equality would be when in case of a fight, my son and the girl are both dealt with on an equal footing.

How do I explain my fear to the boys? How do I tell them that the road to true equality will be steep? Do I want them to be wary?

I have always talked to my sons candidly. They know what it was like for me to bicycle to school, constantly looking over my shoulder. They know the part-time helper's bruises were not because she slipped and fell. They have heard the stories of their great-grandmother fighting all odds to get into a male-dominated profession. They know where my fear comes from. So it was time for me to step out of the car and take my words back.

As I hugged my son and apologised to him for having said what I did, I felt a burden lift. I promised him that I will stand with him in his fight if he needs me to. Bullies are bullies. Period. His gender doesn't have to be his disadvantage, and hers should not be her shield.

As a woman I know all about the daily struggles of women. As the mother of a son, I can see how an innocent boy can get caught in the crossfire of social justice.

But I also feel hopeful when Vivaan gently puts his hand over mine while I am driving and my grip tightens every time a man overtakes my vehicle with a jeer fixed on his face. They know. Their bubbles do not make them blind to what we go through.

Today Ishaan is much more confident and optimistic. 'Don't worry, Mumma. I think by the time we are older, things will change. We will make them change,' he said.

I sighed and smiled. 'But you are a tiny percentage, Ishaan.'

'We have to start somewhere,' he said, and flashed his signature all-teeth-out smile at me.

Of White Lies and Boring Truths

Our hearts break into a million pieces every time our kids lie to us. We might put on a brave front, but it deeply affects us and makes us question our parenting skills. I grew more miserable when the boys were heading towards their teens, and it seemed sometimes that they would fib their way to adulthood.

Then came a point when I took a step back to reevaluate things. It is always a good idea to pause and reassess. And while we are at it, the best way forward is to start from the basics.

WHY DOES A KID LIE?

- She is ashamed of a situation.
- She is afraid of hurting or angering someone important.
- It is the easiest way out of a tight spot.

- She wants to get something she is craving.
- Simply because she loves a good story.

Adults lie for exactly the same reasons. But when your kid lies, you start judging her and yourself. Being truthful is one of the prime virtues we wish to instil in our kids. So, when we discover that our child has been lying to us, there is deep hurt, raised voices, anger and, sometimes, threats.

Lying starts fairly early. To begin with, a child's ideas of reality and fantasy are all muddled up so switching between the two worlds is fairly natural. Then, as a child grows older and starts perceiving anger or disappointment in the parent's tone, she begins lying to get out of tough situations. 'Who ran a crayon across the wall?' The standard answer would be, 'Not me!' Or, if you are blessed with a child with a great imagination, 'The dragon from next door got a little fairy with him and she did it while we had our tea. Would you like some tea?'

From ages five to ten, a child is eager to please the significant adults in her life. By the time she reaches her preteen years, she is able to understand the complexities of truth—and the consequences of lying—fully well. As teenage rolls in, the reasons are not just limited to saving their skins, or getting that candy, but a whole spectrum of developmental and social reasons. Interestingly, if one were to compare statistics, preschoolers lie more than teenagers!

Lying is not always bad. Young children can cook up elaborate tales. Angela Crossman, who has extensively researched the subject, says, 'Preschoolers with higher IQ scores are more likely to lie.'[7] They are better able to understand the way people's minds function. And ultimately, the ability to lie effectively was also speculated to be linked with good social skills in adolescence.

Even if all lying is not bad, this does not mean that we break into a waltz every time the child churns out some outlandish theory about who didn't flush the toilet after using it. It just means that we do not end up questioning the child's moral values at the drop of the hat.

However, we still want our child to speak the truth as far as possible. How does one do that? We need to start from scratch.

HOW WE CAN HELP OUR KID TO SPEAK THE TRUTH

Do not hurl accusations

'Did you break the cup?' 'No.'

When kids sense accusation and anger, they lie out of fear of an adverse reaction. However, if I were to say, 'Let's clean this up. Broken glass could injure someone. Let's be more careful next time,' the child is not faced with an accusation and has no reason to lie.

Once we eliminate the need to lie, we start paving the way for honesty. The boys never lie about marks at home. When they score poorly, there is no shouting or punishments. We analyse where we went wrong, and then figure out a plan for the future. As a parent, my job is to make sure they stick to the plan later on and not use it as an escape route.

Be consistent

There always have to be consequences for unacceptable behaviour. Whatever the rules of the household and behavioural expectations, the child needs to know that they should be consistently adhered to. And in the event of lapses, the consequences, too, need to be consistent.

Lying and misbehaviour are two separate issues and consistency of reaction is essential for both. The consequences could range from letting the child face the situation to taking privileges away; they just have to be consistent.

Let your kid learn from her choices

We do not like our children getting a raw deal at school. We want them to be stars, liked by teachers. So, if the child refuses to do her homework, we threaten, cajole, and ultimately force her into doing it.

A better way would be to let her make a decision and go to school without her homework. Best-case scenario: She learns her lesson the very first time. Worst-case scenario: She lies to the teacher and gets out of a tough spot. However, in the long run, the child will learn the hard way once the work piles up!

Acknowledge and praise

If your child owns up to doing something wrong, praise her for her honesty. This tells her that she will be okay if she comes clean. Go a step further and help her deal with the situation if required.

If we shout at a child for telling the truth, the child concludes that telling the truth isn't all that it's cracked up to be. And she may lie the next time.

Don't overdo the praise though. Making a celebration out of an honest act will diminish the gravity of the situation. Balance is the key.

Distinguishing between lying and creativity

Lying requires creativity. However, if we come down heavily on the child for cooking up an elaborate story, we risk harming creative thought. Hear the tall tale patiently and then appreciate the child's *storytelling* ability by saying, 'That is a fantastic story! Would you like to write it down?' A little later, ask, 'Now would you like to share what really happened?' The child understands that we know that it is a story and are not accepting it as truth, but instead are appreciating her creativity.

👍 Remember the developmental stage

Sitting a toddler down and telling her the merits of being truthful will just make her sleepy. The parent needs to have some awareness of moral development stages, cognitive changes, and motivations to lie, in order to deal with lying in an age-appropriate manner.

As a thumb rule, moral lectures never work. Nor does punishment. At each stage, the child has different reasons for lying. A deeper understanding of these reasons prepares us to deal with the situation better.

👍 Be vigilant

Is the child consistently lying about one particular situation? Get to the bottom of it. Rather than lamenting that she is lying to you, ask yourself why she lied in the first place. The child could be in deeper trouble than we realise. From low self-esteem to external threats, there could be many factors at play. As parents, we need to figure out the reason and deal with it.

👍 Practice what you preach

On the one hand, we lecture the child about being truthful and, on the other, we lie through our teeth on the phone trying to get out of a dinner invitation. Children learn through observation.

The boys know that I do not lie. So, if I commit to taking them somewhere they want to go, I make sure that we go.

And if I threaten to throw their toys in the dustbin in case another sibling fight breaks out, I act on it. When children see adults honouring their word, chances are they will learn to do the same.

A child who lies doesn't make us bad parents and nor does it scar the child's character. If it did, then going by the number of times we lied as kids, we would be a generation of immoral criminals.

At most, lies are a warning signal for us to change our approach. And if we are able to do that, our children learn to take problems head-on rather than hide behind half-truths. Lying is not the end of the world. It is merely the beginning of comprehension of the world and its ways. It is learning by making mistakes. And that form of learning can never go wrong.

Cultivating Empathy

Many years ago, we visited my grandfather who had significantly changed because of Alzheimer's. Ishaan, who was about six then, hugged him, and Nana, being fond of kids, played with him for a while. Nana had a dinky car that Ishaan wanted to play with, but he refused to part with it. Ishaan looked a little disappointed but did not throw a tantrum.

'I am sorry about that, Ishaan,' I tried consoling him.

'It's okay, Mumma. That's his toy. I hate sharing my toys too. Next time I'll get my cars too. Then we can play properly.'

Vivaan's friend shrieked in excitement for a whole minute when he called him. I could hear him through the phone. His mom took the phone away and told him, 'Sorry beta! He has never received a call from a friend before.'

Vivaan grinned as he returned my phone after a while.

'Who were you calling?' I asked.

'That was Atharv.' He hesitantly added, 'He is a little off.'

'Off? What do you mean? Differently abled?' I was gearing up to give him a lecture.

'Ah, yes. That is what I was looking for. I hate it when kids call him "off" at school. He is not a switch.' Vivaan grinned and added, 'I remembered you talking about it but I muddled it up and told the kids that the right term is "differentially impaired". No wonder they laughed!'

I sighed in relief. He remembered. Mistakes like that can be corrected. Attitudes are tougher to change. 'So what makes him different?'

'I don't know the details. I heard the teachers talking, and they said he was injured as a kid and the blow damaged his brain. He has trouble focussing in class, gets very excited and loud. Oh and he loves making lists.' He was getting visibly tired of the interview so I stopped.

That was a year back. They are now good friends, and I hear his name often.

I asked him once if he finds it challenging to be friends with Atharv.

He thought for a few moments and said, 'It is difficult, because sometimes he can be really inappropriate. The other day, he kept asking me to help him hook up with a girl! It got a bit out of control because the girls overheard. It was embarrassing.' He paused and added, 'I snubbed him for the rest of the day and I think he understood. But he is nice to me. Believe me, nice classmates are a rare find!'

'So you are friends because he is nice to you?'

He looked scornful but answered patiently. 'Mumma, I was friends with him way before I discovered that he is nice. He knows so much about cars. And he doesn't show off like a lot of my classmates. We just hit it off instantly. That's all.'

The boys never cease to amaze me. Vivaan was able to figure out that it is okay to be different, and it is fine to be annoyed with his friend based on his behaviour instead of letting things slide out of pity. And Ishaan found common ground with my ailing Nana despite their vast age gap.

As parents, we want our kids to learn empathy. Empathy forms the foundation of pro-social behaviour that the child needs to learn in order to build strong relationships and strengthen the community he lives in. We cannot focus on the child's academic abilities and assume that he will turn out to be a good human being as well. Getting a high grade in maths doesn't ensure that; cultivating empathy, however, just might.

Empathy is too complex to understand as it is often confused with sympathy or even pity. In pity, there is an element of superiority—which could just be that of not being in that difficult situation. When you tut-tut on seeing a rickshaw-puller sweat it out, that is pity. When one feels sympathy, there is a greater sense of sharing the sorrow or troubles of another. Empathy implies a deeper identification with and understanding of another's situation, feelings, and motives. When we are able to feel what the other person is feeling, truly understand what he is going through, and make the whole experience about him rather than our own distress, we are empathising.

Empathy is not easy to cultivate. I say 'cultivate', since it is not as instinctive as fear or joy, and is perhaps rare in an increasingly intolerant world.

HOW TO CULTIVATE EMPATHY

👍 Model well

The first form of learning for any child is from observing her parents. We cannot expect our child to be empathetic towards others if she sees us treat people poorly, or ignore their points of view. A smile and a thank you to the server at the restaurant, a small conversation about her life and concerns with the lady who comes to clean your house, and little gestures to make the people around us, especially the ones working for us, comfortable go a long way in teaching the child to care.

👍 It all begins at home

Anything can upset kids—not being able to find 'that' t-shirt, a friend who threw sand at them, disagreements with parents. At times like these, if we are able to understand their point of view, and convey to them that we understand, we are teaching them empathy. It tells them that we empathise, and it might enable them to do likewise and see the parents' point of view as well.

👍 Small things matter

When Ishaan was in fifth grade, there was a new student in class.

'Do you remember your time when we changed schools last year?' I asked.

He stuffed his face with the last chocolate that I had hidden in the fridge and said, 'I can never forget! The worst bit was that I had no one. Everyone was already friends and knew each others' names but no one knew me. I hated going to school. Then I met Siddarth!' He beamed.

Then it suddenly struck him. 'Mumma! I'll be Siddarth for him! Only he doesn't need to take a month to find me!'

The following day, he launched into a monologue without even dumping his bag on the floor. 'Mumma, all I had to do was look at him and smile! He came and sat next to me. And I gave him my maths and English notebooks so that he can finish the work he missed.'

One doesn't have to make world-changing, grand gestures to leave a mark on young minds.

👍 Give out the right message

What we say to our children each day matters. When we say, 'All that matters for us is your happiness', we are giving them a myopic, selfish vision of happiness. On the other hand if we say, 'It is important for us to be nice to others and always be happy', we are telling them that happiness is not only about ourselves, but also concerns others.

👍 Provide opportunities to exercise empathy

This can be as small as telling a story to the helper's kids, or helping them out with their homework. Basically, we need to be aware of the people around us and their needs, and we need to figure out how we can be of use. Again, if parents set an example, kids follow automatically.

In November 2016, the boys saw me struggle to pay bills, since there was a cash shortage after demonitisation. A few weeks later, I finally managed to get some cash. On our way back, Vivaan asked in a smaller-than-usual voice, 'Mumma, can we afford a cup of ice cream now?'

I smiled and said, 'We can go to the ice cream parlour in the next block.'

He said, 'Ma, can we buy it from a street vendor? You said yesterday that the daily wagers and the small vendors must be going through a tough time. I doubt that he has any cash. Look, he doesn't even have any customers.'

👍 Books—always

Books can be the starting point of discussions, and are especially helpful in gaining a better understanding of humankind, which is the starting point of empathy.

When the boys read Zainab Sulaiman's *Simply Nanju*, it gave us a lot to discuss. Similar emotions were felt when they read R.J. Palacio's *Wonder*. Another book that broke a dam of sorts with Ishaan was Himanjali Sankar's *Talking of Muskaan*. We talked a lot about how people's sexuality influences the way people behave with them, and what they in turn would be feeling. More recently, *Welcome to Nowhere* by Elizabeth Laird has helped Vivaan understand what it is like to be a refugee from a war-torn country.

Grades do not ensure happiness. Neither does material success. However, character strengths such as empathy definitely set us off on the path towards inner peace and happiness.

For Your Bookshelf

Stand in My Shoes by Bob Sornson
The One and Only Ivan by Katherine Applegate
Talking of Muskaan by Himanjali Sankar
Last Stop on Market Street by Matt de la Peña, illustrated by Christian Robinson
Simply Nanju by Zainab Sulaiman
The Invisible Boy by Trudy Ludwig
The Name Jar by Yangsook Choi
El Deafo by Cece Bell
Welcome to Nowhere by Elizabeth Laird
Persepolis by Marjane Satrapi

HOW TO KEEP YOUR CHILD HAPPY

What is his day like?

Oh, he goes for swimming before school, he plays football at school, mental maths in the evening, a dance class after that ... and oh! Self-defence classes over the weekend, an occasional art lesson ...

What about golf?

Do Nothing This Vacation!

'Look at the window, Ma,' a sleepy voice croaked from under the blanket.

'What about it?' I tried to figure out what it was that had grabbed his attention the moment he opened his eyes.

'The dust motes seem to be dancing to the sun's music.'

We spent the next couple of minutes watching them perform. Vivaan joined in and before we knew it, we had given names to the motes, created their worlds, and also helped them wage a war against the Vacuumosaurus.

The final exams had ended, leaving us in the in-between world for fifteen days. Ishaan was neither in Grade VII nor in Grade VIII, and Vivaan had never really cared which grade he was in, anyway. Life had slowed down. The last-minute revisions, maths practice, and studying at unearthly hours had all faded into a distant memory.

'So? What are you planning to do today?'

Both of them rattled off elaborate plans to complete the tasks they had listed a month before the exams—absurdities like repairing strings with magic, farming worms, perfecting skateboard tricks and more, enough stuff to give any mother a full-blown panic attack. At the end of the day, they failed at most of them, ended up with a few bruises and a lot of mud on their clothes from all the digging they did to find worms, but they went to sleep, thinking of alternative strategies for the next day.

I smiled as I scrunched up yet another leaflet advertising a short fifteen-day course for kids to improve their sketching abilities before the new session started. The boys were at peace in the in-between world, mostly doing nothing. They read when they wanted to, woke up late, went to sleep a bit past the curfew hour and they were happy.

All this translates as freedom to them although their television hours are still restricted and the sports hour still mandatory. They were floating in the blissful nothingness of the 'best days of their lives', as they put it every night after our goodnight hug.

A lot of people scoff at this. Some give me the 'What an irresponsible parent!' look and some just sigh, 'You have the luxury, thanks to the hours you work. We do not.' Whatever the case, we need to figure out ways to give the children some time to do nothing.

WHY KIDS SHOULD DO NOTHING

👍 Encourages resourcefulness

Children never actually get bored. They might whine that they are to get hold of the television remote or phone, but if denied, they will find ways to entertain themselves. Vivaan built some of the most complicated catapults using ice-cream sticks, rubber bands and Sellotape while he was getting 'bored'.

Creativity springs from autonomy

If parents plan the child's day down to the last minute, it leaves little scope for the kids to think freely, to discover what inspires them and ultimately, to discover their passion.

Learning coexistence

When there are no rules, kids have to devise their own guidelines and negotiations and, in the process, learn to coexist with the peers or siblings, whoever their partners in crime may be.

Time to experiment and discover

When they have limited and random resources at their disposal, kids fine-tune their decision-making skills, discover things that interest them and may even engage in activities that they might want to pursue later. Ishaan started doodling simply to kill time. Now, he is creating comic books, and plans to learn sketching.

The best stress buster

In a world where scholar badges are missed by 0.2 per cent, sports teachers give graded evaluations, and there are reports of children not getting into colleges despite having scored 98 per cent, there will be stress.

Parents need to unplan a little, let go some more, and set kids free. We structure our kids' days with the best of intentions—we want to maximise learning, hone skills, and work towards a secure future. But in our focus on a bright future, we neglect the present.

Unplanned days give the children time to unwind, regroup, and reenergise, to stretch, breathe and cope.

I stepped into their room one afternoon after college. It looked like a war zone. One corner was a tented battlement area with armies of action figures lined up. The floor was carpeted with Lego pieces, colour pencils, shredded paper, books and more. In another corner were the two boys and their friend huddled up with a book each.

'Mumma!' That was about the only word that I could make out. Each launched into his own account simultaneously. They were happy. They had caught an earthworm but let it go after a while. Vivaan has figured out that he wants to be a 'proper' origami artist, and Ishaan a cartoonist. Tomorrow, as another day gets struck off from their 'nothing calendar', the story might change completely. In this in-between world, they are flourishing, discovering themselves, and taking a fresh look at the world around—while doing nothing.

Every morning, I sip tea outside while the garden is being watered. The boys run about, getting all wet from the hosepipe, and then lie down in the soaking grass for some time.

This morning, as this ritual was happening, a van crammed with kids stopped near the house. Most of them looked bored, some grumpy and two were busy pulling each other's hair. The door slid open, another kid jostled for space as he got in and the door slid shut. Ah! The summer camp kids.

There are so many summer camps for kids—personality development, sketching, dancing, singing and sports, all crammed into three hours, a small room, complimentary transport and a neat amount of money. Depending on the amount charged, there can also be robotics, celebrity theatre workshops and football camps with big-name European soccer clubs.

One year, I just decided to pause the boys' personality development' for forty-five-odd days. My boys were not going to get any more intelligent, confident or skilful that summer—and, as it turned out, any summer since.

I used to pack the boys off to summer camp regularly. But as I look back, I see it as a royal waste of time from their perspective. If summer vacations are as regimented as school, then what's the point?

What summer camps did we go to, as kids? And did we get bored? And haven't we turned out fine in spite of 'wasting' our summers? I remember reading books from Mum's library, playing in the freshly dug-up foundations of houses under construction, aimlessly cycling with a group of friends ... It was pure fun. That is mandatory for any child during holidays—fun.

Ideas often come to people when they're 'doing nothing'.[8] I am not only a believer of this line of thought, but also a witness.

When I checked on them one afternoon, I found one with an elaborate army of action figures—some with missing limbs and some with no head—ready to charge on the alien ship parked near the door. The other was sitting in a carton he found upstairs, and was drawing shapes inside it.

'Spaceship, eh?' I asked trying to sound smart.

I got a disgusted look. 'Time machine.'

'Where are you off to?'

'Dinosaur land!' Their faces were filled with excitement at the possibilities.

By the time they went to bed, the boys had debated

whether the butterfly in the garden was a monarch or not, figured out the faulty aerodynamics of a new paper model of a plane, played a few 'innings' of cricket, made secret potions, read books, told me sick, slimy facts about bugs, fossils and what not, listened to music, played football, and had had a dozen or so fist fights with each other.

Let your child choose. If the camps are his thing, if he wants to learn something specific, go for it. If not, then what's wrong with chasing frogs, running after butterflies, rolling in mud, reading random books and, well, building a time machine?

Learning Respect, From Scratch

I felt violated. We all have, at different points in our lives—by the guy who just sped past on a cycle and tried to grope us, by that pervert who hangs on to the railing in the bus and can never maintain his balance while standing next to a girl, by the group of men standing near the paan shop at the corner who can't help leering at any person of the opposite sex walking by. We have all been violated as we grow older, warier and wearier. But that day was different. I felt violated all over again. Violated and vulnerable.

Somewhere, as we grow older, stereotypes about the perpetrators get fixed in our heads. We start attributing it all to a certain 'type' of men—the ones on the street. We also start believing that education is what separates the animals from the 'real men'.

I am a mother of two boys—fifteen and thirteen years old. They go to one of the best schools in town. They come from a stable, middle-class family. So, by that logic, the boys should be fine. And so should their friends. After all, they, too, are receiving the same education, and come from similar families.

But all that changed one day, two years ago. Ishaan came up to me and mumbled, 'I want to talk to you about something.' The confusion was apparent on his face. 'Two boys in my class have a crush on our teacher.'

'Ah. That is a normal part of growing up ...'

'No, that is not the disturbing part,' he interrupted me. 'They were planning to run down the corridor, and start shoving each other when the teacher got close to them. They intend to "accidentally" bump into her.' His forehead was creased.

'Mumma, they said, "We'll end up touching something." It sounded wrong, Ma. I don't know if I can be friends with them anymore.'

For a few moments, my mind was flooded with all the times I had gone rigid, and had been ready to elbow someone while in a crowd.

I hugged Ishaan, and told him that I was proud of him. That I was glad he felt disturbed. That this is the worst breach of respect.

I felt ridiculous for being so naïve and assuming that education was the shield required to stop turning little boys into the guys we shrink away from. We parents are content with scholar badges, straight As and the odd gold medals that come our way. Do we ever sit and talk about gender sensitisation? Do we lead by example? Do we discuss our own experiences as women? We have assumed that there will be violators but it will never be our sons, because they are protected by the kind of schools and families they come from.

Our job is not done with putting our kids in great schools and fulfilling their material needs. Ours is an ongoing job of keeping the dialogue going, of sensitising the children, of discussing our own feelings towards any form of violation that we might have faced or seen.

I know it is tough, but it is worth it. A boy who knows that women are more than objects is less likely to bump into his teacher so that he can feel her up. A boy who sees his mother being respected may extend the same courtesy to girls in his class. We need to extend education beyond books and grades. Sometimes, we need to simply talk to children to make them more human—talk, not preach.

Help! It's a Teenager

I am a deer caught in the headlights of a superfast train. At least that is what it feels like now that there are two teenagers at home. Nothing prepares you for the tantrums, rebellion, and sometimes, the isolation. I have licked the developmental psychology books clean, taught about adolescence being the 'storm and stress' period to a class full of nodding undergraduates, and doled out advice to parents wound up tighter than a guitar string. But now that the adorable boys have cracked voices and moody dispositions, and are turning into ruthless tyrants in not-quite-full-sized bodies, I am standing on unsure ground.

I try to stay connected, to keep up with the changes, and to maintain a general state of placidity. Here is what has helped me keep calm and mommy on:

THINGS TO KEEP IN MIND WHILE RAISING A TEEN

👍 Selective independence

Teenagers need to be free and have the power to make some decisions. The boys and I have a rule that they will always play one sport, but they get to choose which one. I call it selective independence, which simply means that they get to exercise choice within the limits laid down by the parent. I find it more practical than absolute parental control, or the other extreme—limitless freedom.

👍 Set boundaries

Boundaries are comforting. Studies have revealed that children who grow up in moderately controlled environments with certain ground rules are less stressed and better adjusted. The dos and don'ts, when implemented within reasonable limits, offer a sense of security and order.

👍 Keep the communication going

No notes in the lunch box! A love note from mum sticking out from the bag is even worse than school trousers with a malfunctioning zipper.

When Vivaan started senior school two years ago, he was apprehensive. I left a note pinned to the soft board in his room: 'Dude, sixth grade is tough but doable. You know where to head when and if trouble finds you.' The note is still up there.

There are times when seeing eye to eye becomes impossible. That is when the 'You and I' journal comes in handy. We write about our actions, words, apologies, love, and even that awesome book we read, to each other. Writing things out, instead of having high-pitched fights, has made communication stronger.

It is normal for teenagers to occasionally withdraw or

cut down on communication. Accusing your child of shutting you out of his life will not solve anything. Go for lunch together, or on any outing of his choice. Talk about your day, ask about non-controversial stuff, and just get the conversation flowing. No lectures, no interrogation, just plain fun talk—to get back into the habit of communicating.

Do not advise

Parents feel that it is our our duty to dole out advice. Sometimes, it gets difficult for me to resist. But we have to try. The moment we start telling them what to do, we are telling them that they are incapable of working out a solution. An honest discussion with the child will be more helpful.

Never dismiss the teenager's problems as ridiculous. It could be a big deal to her that her partner didn't talk to her all day, or that she witnessed a fight between two boys. Listen. Do not be dismissive or judgemental about it.

Involve your child in your problems

The boys once came with me to a children's home for a storytelling session. They were excited about the session since I had discussed it with them, had taken their opinions seriously and had assigned them jobs. They ended up being very helpful. I praised them in very precise words. Ambiguous statements like 'good job!' do not really hit home. A better way of putting it would be, 'I truly appreciate your help. You were very patient with the younger lot.' The idea is to be specific and to acknowledge the good things they do.

Teenagers have many skills. To give your teenager responsibility in household work or to involve them in your work shows that you value their intelligence and ability.

👍 Provide varied experiences

I try to provide the boys with as many varied experiences as possible. No, this is not to make their résumés look good. It is to help the boys discover new things they like. A pop-up-card-making workshop led to Vivaan getting interested in paper crafts.

Doing things for the sheer pleasure of experiencing something new has helped us find common ground. Not everything is supposed to have academic relevance—some build character and lead to memorable moments. And some are just things we have fun doing together.

👍 Do not take it personally

Sometimes, one of the boys will stomp out of the room, declaring, 'Life is unfair. You do not understand!' That's when one wants to run away, throw something and howl—all at the same time.

I am learning to not take it personally. It is not about me. It does not reflect on me as a parent. It is the teenage cocktail of hormones, feelings, turmoil, stress, and immaturity. Anger begets anger. I try to remember that I love my son. I take a walk, wash my face and think out a suitable response. Once things have calmed down, make sure that the child understands that rudeness is not permissible.

Each teenager is different. Some things might work for you, and some might not. Just remember that we were once teenagers too. We gave our folks grief too. Our parents have mercifully forgotten the trouble we got into. So will we.

I am banking on that.

Screen Addicts Anonymous

'It is too hot.'

'I don't like this book.'

'This game is useless.'

'I am bored.'

And then, in unison, 'Why can't we watch TV, Mumma, why?'

'Because the weather is so dry.'

That's the kind of ridiculous reply you have to give after you have spent an hour trying to explain to them how their neurons die when they stare at the TV screen all day long.

The flickering screen is the best babysitter that money can buy. The kids never fight with each other or bring the house down while watching TV, which leaves us time to quietly read a book or take a much-needed afternoon nap. We only wake up if things get out of hand. And I am no different.

One day, about eight years ago, the power cut schedule had been changed and the big bad world had decided that the timings of the kids' shows were not important enough to be considered. The boys were splayed on floor, arms flailing and legs kicking around. And there was a lot of screaming. I noticed that the sofa has developed two neat, round depressions where the vegetables had been rooted.

I yanked out the cable that day. For the next year or so, I developed my jaw muscles because of all the clenching I did. There were protests—from refusing meals, to incessant wailing about my cruelty. For some time, they were convinced that I was not biologically related to them. But I firmly held my ground. And once the dark clouds dispersed, it opened up a bright, new world to them.

HOW TO GET YOUR KIDS OFF TV

👍 Shut it—simple

There is no middle ground. So switch it off.

👍 Explain

This is more like the reading of legal rights—it is mandatory and holds no meaning to the culprit. Tell your child how TV is bad for him. He won't understand. But you can rest easy having done the right thing.

👍 Hold a peace meeting

Give your child selective power. On weekends, he can catch one show.
In the case of my boys, they have to agree on and let me know. Two birds with one stone: It gives them confidence

that some things are still in their hands and they are forced to cooperate with each other. Ta da!

👍 Stick to it

You know how rehab works. There will be withdrawal symptoms ranging from tantrums to questioning your parenting skills. Take a deep breath and clench your jaw. If you relent once, you are telling them that whining works. In no time, you'll be reduced to a slot machine—keep pushing the levers and you will eventually hit jackpot.

👍 Give alternatives

No kid can stay bored for a long time. Slip in alternatives on the sly. Do not tell your child the purpose, or he will not even touch it in protest. Just leave stuff lying around, feign ignorance and wait for him to take the bait. Books are my favourite form of bait.

👍 Bring in the stars

Reinforcement always works. Praise or reward the alternatives your child explores. But do not overdo it. Children are smart, and see through devious adult fumblings. The books that have been read, the hours in the park, and a whine-free day—you need to pick the behaviours to reward, which will earn them stars. A pre-decided number of stars earned can be exchanged for something your child desires. And please, do not exchange the stars for extra TV time!

It has been more than eight years, and there are still days when I hear a distant grumble about how the boys cannot watch their favourite shows all the time. The screen time definition has expanded to include the Wii and the computer. Exceptions are made for homework assignments that require research on the internet.

High Score

We had gone to watch a movie recently. The two teenagers of the family seated in the row in front of us spent the entire duration of the movie mindlessly tapping on their phone screen, playing some game.

A few days after that, I met a toddler's mother, who uses her phone as a soother. 'Whenever my daughter cries, I give her my phone. She knows how to swipe to get to the next picture.' The mum's eyes shone with pride for having birthed a genius.

We are to take a vacation in the hills soon, and the boys are not allowed to carry any gadgets. They have packed in Keri Smith's *Wreck This Journal* to fill up during the vacations, a couple of books to read, and are looking forward to trying their hand at photography during our break. They will have lots of time to get bored, whine a bit, and then try different things to fight the boredom. Taking away the gadgets opens up a much larger world to them.

I have explained to the boys why screens are bad for them, and I hide the gadgets. No wonder I am perceived as a dictator! It sometimes gets tough to say no all the time, but I am fairly thick-skinned, and consistency is my middle name. They are allowed to play video games very sparingly—in fact, so sparingly that they forget about it most of the time. There is also an old cellphone at home but they are fairly clear about its purpose: to be used in case of emergency. Games and messaging do not qualify as an emergency yet.

Much has been written about the ill effects of excessive screen time. I see kids walking around, with their unblinking eyes fixed on a screen all the time. I am sometimes questioned about how I manage to keep them off screens.

It is always tough to swim against the tide, even more so for children. The boys have classmates who mock them for their ignorance about the latest video games. I believe in arming them with a thick skin rather than the latest technology. Yes, I use unfair means, but then all is fair in love, war and mommyhood.

Straitjacketed Childhood

Is it fair to straitjacket childhood? To put blinkers on your child, lead her to the starting gate and expect her to run like a champion racehorse?

The queue to meet the maths teacher snaked right up to the door. 'What are you doing to prepare you child for IIT?' asked the mother standing in front of me.

I spun around to see whom she was talking to. Turns out she was referring to me.

'Err, my son has just turned thirteen.'

'Yes, so is he not going to FIT-JEE?'

'Fit what?'

She gave me an are-you-for-real look. Thankfully, her turn to be grilled by the teacher was next and I was saved.

A friend messaged recently telling me that her toddler would soon be joining music classes, and how she was told that she is already behind by six months—something about cognitive enhancement.

Another kid I know has his feet in as many different boats as possible in the name of 'channelising energies'.

All this unnerves me. I stand back and question myself. Am I an adequate parent?

Is there a defined parenting path? Have I ensured optimal levels of cognitive functioning? Have I charted their trajectories? I think the answer to all three questions is in the negative. I do not yet have my own trajectory in order! So, I certainly cannot determine that of my boys' for them.

During exams, when parents and children both lose sleep, all entertainment is banned, and conversations focus on percentages, my house is pretty much as usual. In my defence, I honestly tried to get the boys to study as if their life depended on it. But I might as well confess that my efforts lacked a certain conviction. And I met with little success: I couldn't prevent the boys from reading their choice of fiction, or making origami and scoubidou string rings. I have not forgotten that I never took exams seriously, either. And I seem to be doing fine. So how do I pretend? I cannot. Hence, I give up. I can't be that parent.

I had told Ishaan that he wasn't studying the way he was 'supposed to'. Then in an introspective moment, realisation hit me—who was I to judge his system? For all I know, it might work. Just because convention demands that he study for hours at a stretch does not mean that his system of getting up from the desk every twenty minutes doesn't work. He was working out his method. An apology was in order.

I tried to be the mom of advertisements—the one who worries, helps the child write furious notes, finishes assignments, and stays awake all night to make hot drinks.

I failed. How long can you pretend, after all? I was never an organised student and I feel a bit hypocritical trying to be outraged if they are not. So, I leave them to their own devices. They study—sometimes at the last minute, and sometimes in a more disciplined manner than I ever had.

When I get after them, am I ensuring success, or am I preventing them from learning from failure? Does my relentlessness motivate them to do better? I think not.

So, I made my decision: I am going to let the boys make their decisions. Success or failure—it is going to be theirs. That is how they will learn. A huge part of exams, I believe, is not categorising us according to the marks we get, but to gauge our strengths and weaknesses. The purpose of exams is to pave the way forward, not to get flogged for getting half a mark less than the highest, or for that matter failing.

I hear fellow parents cite reasons—fierce competition, financial security and the necessity of rising above the crowd—for the strict path that they have chosen for their children. Also, at some level, they seem to distrust the abilities of their own kids, whom they otherwise consider smart: 'What do kids know? Parents have to decide for them what they want to be.'

But being responsible doesn't mean taking every decision for your child, or making choices for them, or forcing your dreams on them. Being responsible means helping them arrive at decisions, letting them know you will stand by their choices and respecting their dreams. Being responsible definitely means accepting their mistakes, and helping them learn their own lessons from them. If as a parent, I am able to teach them how to deal with successes and failures, and how to be persistent in following their dreams, I'd label myself as responsible.

Competition has always existed. Financial insecurities will never go away. And the dream of seeing your child shine in a crowd is understandable. But is it fair to turn your child's life into a never-ending series of study times, grades, and arguments with teachers? Hypertension, anxiety disorders, depression and suicide rates are rising at an alarming rate among adolescents and teens.

I totally support extracurricular activities for children. But to enrol a child in a professional art class because he doodled in preschool is ridiculous. I never enrolled them for music classes when they were toddlers even though they swayed and hummed to whatever was playing in the car. So far, I have not noticed any cognitive disadvantages.

The boys are not going to any IIT coaching centre. They are torn between career choices. Toymaker or dessert chef? Game developer or writer? It is a tough decision.

So You Want to Be a Tiger Mom?

'So, what kind of school do you prefer?' This was an elegant woman at a fancy party.

'Err … the educating kind?'

There was some muscular movement on her face that suggested she was clenching her jaw and her right eyebrow was raised to reflect contempt.

'What *kind* of education?'

It was clear that she was looking for some kind of a well-thought-out reply.

'There is more than one?'

She rolled her eyes, mumbled about getting her empty glass refilled and moved away.

I get the jaw-clenching, eye-rolling and eyebrow-lifting a lot. Because I answer like that a lot.

It is better to feign ignorance than justify my stance. Tiger Moms! Somewhere in the Sunderbans, a tiger mum just winced at that misnomer. She doesn't push her cubs to swim an extra length or run an extra mile. She just sits idly and watches her cubs explore life, always keeping an eye out for danger and putting them in their place when they get to be a pawful. So, by that definition, I guess I am a Tiger Mom. But, if you go by the popular reference, I fall more in the Dinosaur Mom category, more specifically the herbivorous kind.

A few years ago, Ishaan used to participate in junior golf tournaments. I can only imagine how unnerving it must have been for him to deal with the pressure, when I, the tough grown-up bystander, used to get palpitations merely listening to the mums there. They came armed with plastic smiles and a steely gaze that could freeze the marrow in your bones, and talked of competitions, three-hour lessons and elaborate warm-up routines.

'What do you do to get him to do better?' they would ask me with great seriousness.

'Err … let him play?'

They would roll their eyes, clench their jaws and move away. Phew!

It does get difficult to stay unaffected when you have frenzied parents all around you. And there you are, with a mug of coffee and two boys who mostly read, sometimes write and indulge in free play at the local park if they aren't playing with their five dogs. That doesn't mean they don't do anything else. They do play their fair share of sports but never have I walked up to the coach and asked him when they can play 'professionally'. As long as they keep those muscles moving, I am satisfied.

The quintessential Tiger Mom would find my sons unmotivated, directionless children with a bleak future. But how boring to know at twelve what you'd want to be at forty! It is delightful to see their ambitions change from an astronaut to an artist to a comic-book illustrator and then settle on being a bookstore owner for a while, before it changes again.

When I was in college, our lecturer had told us, 'There is enough space for everyone in this world and there is absolutely no point in thrusting our own dreams on our kids.' In pursuit of that ephemeral 'bright future', is it fair to push my child to study a particular subject or pursue a sport? What does a bright future mean, anyway? Are we feeling dissatisfied with our own lives and making our real or imagined failures stepping stones to make them lead a life we failed to achieve?

This sense of competition starts early. When one kid turned one and a mother exclaimed to me, 'Hasn't he started walking yet? Mine walked at ten months!' It is admittedly hard as a parent to not feel even the slightest pang when one's child is outshone by another. How do I remain immune when I hear other moms brag about their little ones' skills and medals? Or when I see another child outshine mine in a debate? And it is difficult not to feel a little twinge of concern when other mothers say, 'German? Why did you allow him to study that? Sanskrit is far more scoring.' Sanskrit could be scoring but my ten-year-old wanted to study German and that was a good enough reason for me.

Psychologists across the globe are presenting large amounts of data indicating that happy, fulfilled children go on to have contented, joyful lives.[9] This happiness comes from exercising strengths of character, and not mindless mugging up of textbooks, unless that is something that gives them joy! The point is that they ought to feel joy when they compete in those maths classes or dance competition.

Each day, I question myself—am I doing the right thing? But the loud gales of the boys' laughter drown out that query. Something tells me that we are okay. The boys are doing well at school, they have read more books than I ever laid my hands on, they are mostly respectful, barring the times when the hormonal surges happen and most of all, the stress in their lives is still limited to dog-eared pages or broken toys. They are compassionate and never hesitate to question. What else can I ask for?

So, as Tiger Moms continue to claw and tear ahead, pulling their children along relentlessly, we Dino Moms smell the roses that the little ones got for us, with bonus hugs thrown in.

Outsourcing Creativity

In front of the teacher's desk in Grade II was a perfect folder—handmade paper, straight lines, beautiful origami flowers tacked on with the symmetry of a military garden. At the bottom of the folder were scribbled a smiley and an A+. In the far corner of the Grade II classroom was another project. It had a kilo of glitter powder on it, three crooked stars, and the pages were cut in a series of jagged lines, making the edge look like a pathway deep in the jungle. It had a sad-looking B-. This was Vivaan's project.

Vivaan grumbled on the way home, 'Everyone gets their projects done by their mums. Only you insist that I have to do it myself.'

They still do their own projects. Neither boy expects me to help them with their holiday homework. They had been told early on and often enough that it is their homework, not mine. Sometimes they grumble, 'This is a waste of time. We can easily get this from the store. Everyone does that.' Sometimes, I explain all over again the logic behind doing things independently, but many times, I just ignore their pleas. Yeah, I can be a witch.

It does sadden me, nevertheless, that parents fall into the perfection trap. And can't the teachers see through it all? When a child gets an A+ on work that is screaming 'store-bought!' or 'made by parents!', he learns to value grades, and not the work required to get them. Is that really what we want our children to learn? That hard work is overrated? That as long as you are getting credit, it doesn't matter how you get a thing done?

WHAT DOES YOUR KID LEARN FROM PROJECTS?

How to research

When presented with a project, the child will use her mind and brain and organisational abilities to plan it all out. Sometimes the plan will work and sometimes it will end in a huge mess. But the mess that she makes today will teach her something for tomorrow.

How to execute

At the execution stage, there will be many blunders. Unless these are life-threatening or could result in the house being burnt down, continue to be uninvolved. I stay at a watchful distance but do not interfere, much to the disapproval of the boys.

How to finish on time

My boys have managed to finish every single time. The work might not have straight lines, might depict outlandish ideas and might scream C-, unlike the manicured, assembly-line projects. But these are their babies. And over the years, they have learnt to disregard the grades and enjoy the process.

👍 Creativity

Left to their own devices, the boys use every creative cell to come up with a solution. Yes, it promotes creative thinking. When the parent does it for the child, or when the child walks into a store to buy ready-made projects, these cells shrivel up and die a horrible death.

👍 Self-worth

When a child does something on her own, accomplishes something independently, it instills a sense of pride. It imbues your child with self-confidence that she can take on new things with ease.

👍 Learning to choose

I have always explained to the boys why getting projects from the market is wrong rather than just disallowing it. I prefer standing behind them when they come to a fork in the road and if asked, telling them what each path has in store. They make their own choices. The good part is, because of this freedom of choice, they have not taken a wrong decision so far. They might grumble but they always choose the right path.

👍 Important life lessons

Ultimately, despite their enthusiasm, despite gluing the last dried leaf to their project meticulously, the coveted A+ has so far eluded the boys. Life is unfair. And they learn that each day.

Ishaan trawled the internet and his books for information on blood, and ended up reading way more than he was required to. Vivaan is distressed that he cannot find the thirty new words they have been asked to find in four English chapters. 'I swear I am not showing off, Mumma, but I know these words. They are not new.'

Ishaan, being overexcited because his project was almost done, hugged me one evening, a fairly rare occasion in the teenage chapter.

'Mum? Thanks.'

'Eh?'

'Homework isn't all that bad, you know. Completing the project is way more fun when I dig for stuff. I think I'll attach a slide of blood with my project. So, would you ...'

'No! I am not giving you a drop of my blood.'

'Darn.'

Yeah, well. Sometimes we go overboard.

Analysing the Education System

'What has your son planned? Medical? Non-medical?'

I looked at my almost-fifteen-year-old who was buried in a book, a few tables away. On the chair facing him, the younger one was busy making an intricate Zentangle pattern.

'By the looks of it, neither!'

My friend was suitably horrified. 'You need to direct their minds towards something.'

'Mould their brains, box them and label them as an engineer or a doctor, you mean?'

She sighed and shook her head. 'They don't know what's best for them. You have to tell them what they want to become.'

At times like these, I smile and retreat. I am no revolutionary. If she is happy putting blinkers over her children's eyes, so be it. I would, however, like to believe that my sons have enough intelligence and self-awareness to be able to figure it all out, when the time comes.

QUESTIONING EDUCATION

Why school?

School followed by college are seen as logical stages in a kid's life. We never stop to question the purpose of education. Is it purely to ensure a fat pay cheque? A secure job? Or is it more than that?

I believe that education is a value addition in terms of character building, learning, and widening of horizons. No pay cheque is fat enough if the child grows up into an adult who has no idea about what he wants, or worse, is far away from his dream. Education is meant to give kids wings, not chains.

Who sets the rules?

For some strange reason, all over the world, science is valued over the arts. Who set the rules for what is best for kids?

'He is forever doodling. Does he study as much?'

I looked at Vivaan. 'He manages. He seems to love art though, and can spend endless number of hours making ridiculously detailed artworks.' There was a definite note of pride in my voice.

My inquisitor asked, 'So, which science stream is he going to opt for in eleventh?'

At that point, Vivaan had just started eighth grade. By the looks of it, he would thrive if he gets to do something creative. So why was there this tendency to send him off to study science?

As a parent, my focus is on providing opportunities that let Vivaan explore his potentials, not persuading him to do something allegedly 'better'. So, we frequent art workshops, and I get art supplies with heart-attack-inducing prices for him. In return, I have a happy, engaged child, who is playing by his own rules.

Are grades what it is all about?

Today's education system is marked by the absence of value-based education. No, I am not referring to moral education classes, I am referring to discovering one's true potential, learning about individual value structures and respecting life in general. On my frequent trips to school I see children being classified according to their grades—topper, average or, worse, a failure! Somewhere, the system assumes a direct correlation between academic excellence and moral character.

The emphasis ought to be on finding the child's character strengths and talents, and helping him harness them. Grades do not determine the child's worth. It is the other way around, and we keep forgetting that.

Are we overemphasising success?

Everyone loves success stories. So, we gently push the failures—the ones who falter—to the back of the line, and forget about them. They get treated as numbers—nothing more. We are teaching our children to either succeed at any cost or get reduced to a nameless shadow.

Instead of condemning failure, we need to teach kids to use failure as the stepping stone to success. A big part of education should be about encouraging children to try diverse things, to deal with failure, to dust their knees when they fall and stand back up again. Without that, true education stays incomplete.

Is it really a straight road?

Like a 'good' Indian girl, I first opted for the medical stream in Grade XI, since my family felt that there should be a doctor in the clan. A year later, I was standing in the principal's office to sign the request form for dropping biology. Another year—and a series of engineering entrance exams later—I ended up studying psychology. Three years later, I was at a fashion design institute. Thankfully, better sense prevailed, and I realised psychology was my calling. Today, I dream of being a full-time writer. Oh, and I am completely happy resetting my goals even today.

Success is not as straightforward as the system has made it out to be. The boys love reading up on the latest research in science as much as they like reading about historians discovering new clues about human civilisations.

We need to encourage flexibility in our education system. Engineers and doctors are not all that the world needs. We need writers, historians and artists too.

As parents, we need to entrust our children with more freedom. Freedom to study the economic conditions of a remote African nation, or fashion trends in the seventeenth century, for that matter. We need to ensure that children get the freedom to choose, dream and be different, if they wish. We need to encourage them to question, to debate, to figure out who they want to be rather than making 'safe' choices for them.

Is Percentage the Definition of Success?

'What do you mean by cut-off percentage?'

I drew a deep breath in and explained the concept to Ishaan.

'So, even above ninety per cent is not good enough?'

Headlines on the front page of the newspaper said that percentages were calculated to the second decimal place. And that cut-offs were in the upper mid-nineties.

These percentages seem to calculate a person's worth down to a number, based on her position relative to the cut-off percentage. They seem to suggest that nothing matters—hobbies, passions, character strengths. If it cannot be graded, it doesn't exist.

Cut-off. It sounds so morose. So mechanical. Ishaan's question reveals what kids feel about the sword that swiftly slices through millions like him, and divides them into the 'above' and 'below' kids. What does 'good enough' mean?

I'll be lying if I said I do not feel scared every year when I see such headlines. Am I making 'wrong' choices? The boys are never asked who scored the highest in a particular test. They have, so far, been straight-A students but I never ask whether they made it to the top. The question is whether they outdid themselves or fell short of their own expectations. And if they did indeed stumble in some test, the focus is not on their failures, but on what to do the next time. Our lives do not revolve around academics.

I have never told them what they ought to become. I encourage them if they want to persue crafts that are deemed 'useless'. We let the scores languish in a corner as Ishaan practices guitar and develops cold feet over his upcoming stage debut. The marksheets lie forgotten as Vivaan eases the last band off the loom to make an intricate dragon out of rubber bands.

I do not let these doubts fill my lungs and cloud my mind for too long. I truly believe in happiness. And happiness cannot be defined by cut-offs alone. However, I am not a revolutionary. The boys are not being trained to break all moulds either. We are attempting to create our own guidelines.

We do not know what the future holds and we don't dwell too much on cut-offs. With each book I put back on the shelf, each Lego piece I pick off the floor, and each artwork I stack away, the answer to my son's question gets clearer.

'Hey!' I walked into the room to see Vivaan finishing an elaborate origami project that he had been absorbed in for the past two hours. Ishaan was examining some slide, the contents of which are best left unknown, under the microscope.

'You asked yesterday whether ninety per cent is good enough?'

Ishaan looked up and nodded. 'Is it?'

'Do you enjoy studying?'

'Yes. Most of it. I mean I love history, chemistry, bits of biology, and now even maths doesn't seem all that bad. Why do you ask?'

'Then it doesn't matter whether ninety per cent is good or bad.'

The confusion on his face deepened. 'Umm? Mum? What if I don't score enough for a good college?'

'If you enjoy the process, if you have fun learning, scores lose their fear factor. It won't matter what the cut-off is … If you know what you enjoy, and if you can work hard to learn everything about it. Cut-offs won't be able to cut your future off from you.'

I do not know how much of this he understands today. But I do hope that both of them realise that marks are not a measure of their worth, hard work is. Their rank doesn't define them, their focus and the joy that they find in their work, does. So, for now, I am going to breathe and not be defeated by the fourth cut-off list that will appear in the newspaper. And as for the boys, I have a feeling that they'll find their way.

Needs vs Wants

'Can I have that pen? It is just ₹500, Ma, and I need it.'

What all is wrong with that sentence? Firstly, the 'just ₹500' is what the guy who washes our car charges for a month's work. Secondly, yes, he needs a pen, but a fifty-rupee pen would do an equally good job.

But your child asking for it is not the problem. The problem is that you usually relent.

It is not about affordability; it is about teaching the child to differentiate between needs and wants. It is also about teaching children to deal with refusal.

Children need to learn the importance of delayed gratification. Simply put, it means that they should acquire the decision-making ability that helps them make a choice to forego something now for the pleasure of being able to have something better later.

WHY IS DELAYED GRATIFICATION IMPORTANT?

👍 Helps develop self-control

Children who are able to accept reasoned arguments and learn to say 'no' to themselves, grow up to be adults with better self-control. According to research, the children who were able to delay gratification when they were four, generally scored higher in academics, exhibited more social competence, and were better at planning and handling stress.[10]

👍 There are links between self-control and intelligence

Intelligence and self-control are deeply related since both originate in the same part of the brain. Saying that self-control leads to better intelligence would be stretching it a bit, but they have been seen to coincide.

👍 Highlights the importance of achieving goals

When we tie wants to goal achievement, chances are that the child will strive to get those rewards, and, in the process, learn a thing or two about hard work, persistence, as well as dealing with failure.

👍 Heightens appreciation

Delayed and rationed gratification teaches the child to appreciate things much more. From the time the boys started buying their own stationery, there are fewer 'thefts' reported, and everything is preserved in prime condition.

👍 Teaches kids about the value of money

In today's highly materialistic world, children need to learn the value of money, as well as its triviality when it comes to achieving true happiness.

An important thing to consider while teaching children to differentiate between needs and wants is that learning is linked to the developmental level of understanding. A two-year-old cannot be expected to wait patiently for hours to get a pat on the back or a candy.

The child's personality, as well as the present physical and mental conditions, plays an important role. If you set out to teach an unwell or an irritated child the importance of overlooking desires, you might find yourself in a puddle of tears.

HOW TO TEACH YOUR CHILD SELF-CONTROL

👍 Model well

Show your child that you are willing to forgo your desires so that the needs of others are met. Also, go shopping with a list. This shows that you carefully thought about what is needed and are not buying on a whim.

👍 Don't give in to tantrums

The easiest route to end a tantrum is to give in. That is also a sure-shot technique to ensure that behaviour is ingrained. Kids rarely grow out of tantrums; they merely remodel it to fit age-appropriate behaviour.

Be sure to *never* give in to tantrums. So, draw in a long breath and wait for your child to get up, so that you can leave the shop without the shouting matches or the customary 'oh, all right, buy it!'

👍 Try to engage in sports or music

Learning music or taking up a sport requires patience and hard work. Neither ensures success and both require complete engagement. Hence, they become excellent tools for teaching the meaning and value of delayed gratification.

👍 Differentiate between needs and wants

Make a list of all the things that your child has, and those he says he needs. Explain to him that needs are things we must have in order to survive. All the other things that we can live without, but would like to have, are wants. Ask him to underline the needs. Once done, discuss why a video game is not a need while food is.

👍 Teach your kid about money

Children as young as four years can understand the value of saving, so it is never too early to teach them about how money works. It is essential that they learn that the ATM machine doesn't magically produce money.

👍 Pay bills together

Take your child with you to pay bills. Talk to him about monthly expenses. Ask him to count out the salary for the house help, the gardener or any other person around the house. This not only helps him understand how much money it takes to keep the house running, but also to appreciate what the salary means to the helpers. The amount that they want for a PSP game might be feeding multiple mouths for a month.

👍 Give your child the opportunity to earn

Your child should be helping out around the house without expecting compensation. But, sometimes, offer him the opportunity to earn money. Fix the amount of money he can make by completing a particular additional task. Compensate fairly—overpaying kills the purpose. An opportunity to earn will teach him the value of money, as well as the joys of financial independence, however limited.

👍 Teach your child to budget

Give your child three jars. Label them: 'Share', 'Save' and 'Spend'. Whenever he earns money from chores or receives money from a doting aunt, place a pre-decided percentage in each jar. Stick to the rule, consistently. For example: sixty per cent could be for saving, thirty per cent for spending and ten per cent for sharing.

👍 Teach your child to compare prices

When your child decides to spend out of his jar, encourage him to compare prices. For example, if we are browsing for books, we buy them at places where we get membership discounts, or online, where there is a good deal thrown in. The boys have realised that they can maximise the power of their money by waiting for the courier guy, who would probably deliver the same book a week later at a lower price.

👍 Set realistic goals

Tie incentives to goals, instead of buying on a whim. That way, your child is motivated to work towards the goal and learns patience and persistence. Discuss with the child to arrive at an attainable goal, so that he does not give up easily.

We are living in materialistic times. As adults, we realise that real happiness is not in our bank balance, the labels on our handbags, or the destinations on our travel tickets. We must teach our children this, because their world might be even more materialistic than ours.

With the ever-growing lists of wants, it is urgent that children realise the futility of money in achieving true happiness, as well as the importance of reining in their impulses. The good news is that it is perfectly doable and we can help them with it.

READING THE WORLD

Do you have a book that teaches maths?

Can you show some books that teach good manners?

Do you have a book that teaches respect for elders?

Are you sure that this book is okay for a fourteen-year-old? I hope there is no lovey-dovey stuff in it ...

...

Ten Myths about Children's Books

'Could you do me a favour? Could you include a book on listening to parents' instructions? My daughter just doesn't listen.'

'No. I tell stories. You be the parent.'

Sometimes conversations do end that curtly.

I narrate stories to children for fun. Yet, a sizeable number of enquiries from parents are about if they can expect improvements in vocabulary and fluency, and whether value education would happen or not. Would it transform the child into a pious, pliant soul? Would it dramatically improve their IQs, and brighten their chances of getting into a top engineering or medical college?

While I am a great believer in the power of books, it seems a bit much to expect all of that from an hour's worth of reading!

Books and children go very well together. If only parents would stop looking for outcomes and utility and let children go off and find books to read as they please. Sadly, many parents do not. Online reading groups get bombarded with queries about books that teach children good manners, the importance of sharing, how not to be afraid of dark, the necessity of studying, the nutritional value of peas, facts about the solar system, and anything else that one can think of.

It is essential that we bust a few myths that are associated with the unassuming objects stacked on our bookshelves, waiting for little hands to find them:

THINGS TO UNLEARN WHILE PICKING BOOKS

The moral of the story is ...

Nothing. Zilch. Moral lessons are best learnt through life experiences. Why drag books into it? Ask any bookseller and they'd burst into tears if they were to recount each time a parent came in asking for books with lessons. Even without life-altering messages, books are engrossing, fun and worthy of being loved. And they might still alter your life.

Pink cover = girl's book

Okay, I hate sparkly covers. Nevertheless, the presence of fluffy bunnies, princesses or any such so-called girly things doesn't determine the gender of the reader. Neither do zombies on the cover make it a boys' book.

There was once a bookstore assistant who smirked at Ishaan's choice and said, 'Arrey, that is a girls' book. Why don't you try this?' She shoved a Hardy Boys in his hands. I gave her an unwelcome lecture, and we never went back to that store. Books know no gender. Period.

There are no boys' books or girls' books. I have grown up reading all sorts of 'boys' books' and my gender identity is firmly in place, thank you.

Age groups are all-important

Fifteen-year-old Ishaan loves picture books. Thirteen-year-old Vivaan's eyes get wider every time he leafs through the wordless picture books. And I usually steal all their books as soon as the courier arrives. 'Age is just a number,' Ishaan once said. 'And books are too big to be bound by numbers.'

While defined age groups can be useful when your child starts reading, don't cling to them for too long. Each child figures out his own course.

In our anxiety to get our children to read books appropriate for their age, we might just extinguish the desire to read. Just as we enjoy all sorts of desserts, from laddoos to gourmet French pastries, each book has its own flavour. It would be boring to eat just one kind of food every day. Let them choose, irrespective of what the bookshelf label says.

Reading fiction is useless

I had once won our team the class quiz. The question that clinched it was, 'Where was the first lighthouse built?'

The answer was Pharos, in Egypt. Source: *Asterix and Cleopatra*.

Reading fiction, apart from being immeasurably fun, provides an excellent opportunity to get curious, learn entirely random facts, and increase vocabulary phenomenally, in addition to a fairly long list of other good stuff. Vivaan had used the word smithereens in a sentence in Grade III. He came back with a smug grin and said, 'I had to explain the meaning of the word to the entire class.'

So expensive—not worth it

Some books seem exorbitantly priced. But they are worth every rupee spent on them. The boys finish a book within a day or two. But they reread, exchange with each other, and reread again a year later. From ridiculously expensive picture books to astronomically priced pop-up books—we save up for them all. Don't let the price get in the way of the wonder in their eyes. If you can afford it, feel lucky, and splurge on books.

The world is flat, with Roald Dahl at one end and Enid Blyton at the other—and oh, Ruskin Bond somewhere in the middle

I love these authors, I really do. But there is a whole galaxy beyond these—with many stars and some meteors and some galactic junk. Our children's reading tends to be largely American or British. There are so many Indian writers to discover—and writers from Europe, Asia, Africa and Australia. Explore. Experiment. You can't go wrong.

The ship has sailed

'My child just never took to reading. It is too late now.'

Once, there was a boy who never really read much beyond a comic here and there. He grew older, got married to the most awesome woman there is, and became a father to two bookworms. He made it clear over the years that books and he just did not get along.

One fine day, he came back with a book. He had been stranded at the airport with nothing better to do. Today, his shelf fills up quicker than mine.

No time to read

Many people argue that academic pressure at school is so great that there is no time to read. This is an excuse offered by non-readers or parents who focus too much on academics.

Ishaan and Vivaan are bang in the middle of final exams. They can be found reading their entirely non-academic books during breaks. The breaks are sometime longer than intended. So far, they have been getting straight As.

Graphic novels are not proper books

From the classics to contemporary fiction, from picture books to graphic novels, every book counts. There are no extra brownie points earned for reading a particular genre.

There are many kids and adults who have read comics and only comics. It is a perfectly valid reading option.

The protagonist sets a bad example for my child

Children are not stupid. If they haven't worn a cape and set out to rescue the world, chances are they will read, and leave whatever they read tucked inside the pages.

Sometimes, it is important to have an honest discussion to understand the choice of words or characters for a book. On reading a particular book, Vivaan said, 'There are some curse words in there.' When my eyebrows shot up, he grinned. 'I am not that silly, Amma! I know the words were needed to build that character and are not to be used. Jeez!'

So relax. If you've been blessed with bookworm children, rejoice and let them be.

Two Teenagers, Picture Books and a Closet

We read books in secret. No, I am not talking about *Fifty Shades of Grey*. We read picture books and enjoy them immensely. It is like an unspoken pact that the boys have with me. I take the entire blame for the swelling numbers of picture books on the bookshelves. They pretend to not care. It is working out well so far. They are teenagers and there is a limit to which you can challenge the teen boundaries of cool and uncool. Reading picture books falls on the uncool side of the boundary. I do not challenge this. They do not need to shout from the rooftop how much they loved a particular picture book. I do that for them.

I don't blame them. They would never hear the end of it if word got out. Thing is, their peers have been systematically conditioned to be in a hurry to grow up. And one of the sad markers is the kind of books one reads. Picture books fall in the diaper-wearing, drooling infant stage. It's still acceptable in preschool.

WHY NOT TO READ PICTURE BOOKS

Waste of money

Picture books are a colossal waste of money, I am told. The child gets done with it within a few minutes. I usually recommend the Yellow Pages, or, better still, the phone directory, to such people—both have plenty of pages, which could take a lifetime to read.

I understand that some picture books are very expensive but to say they are a waste of money is unfair. Picture books are savoured not just for the story—sometimes, there is none. It is the power of words and the pictures together that creates an experience unique to each reader. Besides, they can always be revisited.

Your child will outgrow them soon

Academic prowess and interest do not necessarily go hand in hand. You might come across theories that expound the importance of 'encouraging' a reader by presenting more 'challenging' reads to him. I disagree. The only sure-shot way of encouraging a reader is to surround him with books he loves. The challenges are automatically taken up, as the child starts to swim freely in the world of books. Providing a challenge by thrusting chapter books on him and banning picture books could easily backfire. I have two bookworms at home who are a perfect example of this. There has never been a transition; there only have been additions. So our shelves are full of picture books, chapter books, middle reads, and YA fiction, absolutely not in that order.

Picture books are not just a rung on the reading ladder. There are excellent ones that are layered enough to be enjoyed by all ages. The boys loved chewing on the board books when they were babies. As toddlers, the pictures told them a different story each time they turned the pages. The books also became a weapon in case of a disagreement.

By the time they were in Grade I, they started sticking their chests out in a bid to look older. The picture books started gathering dust. 'They are for babies!' I was told. I continued picking up the ones that I fell in love with, anyway.

Over the past few years, the boys have found their way back to picture books. They read everything, from blood-curdling YA reads like Kevin Brooks' *The Bunker Diary* to their all-time favourite Maurice Sendak's *Where the Wild Things Are*.

They are not yet ready to go against the tide and declare to their peers that they love picture books. So, I do not pull them out of the closet yet. I sit there with them and ogle at the goodness between the pages. These books are a journey for them—with each extra mile, they discover something new.

A few days back, the younger one dreamily looked at the cover of Maurice Sendak's *Where the Wild Things Are*, and declared, 'I wish I had a forest in my room.'

I was reading Nina Sabnani's *A Bhil Story*.

'I can't bring the forest to your room but we *can* paint a tree!' And so we created a ten-foot Pithora tree in his room.

This is what we get from picture books—art transcending the pages and seeping on to the walls of our rooms, and into our hearts.

Oh, and the picture books on their bookshelves?

'They are Mum's. Yeah. She reads all sorts of things.'

Once Upon a Time

'Story?'

'No. Too tired.'

The refusal never had the desired effect. Ishaan, aged two, mistook that as, 'Of course, just get me another book.'

'Dino?'

Shoved in front of my nose was his favourite book on dinosaurs. The next few minutes were spent reading tongue-twisting dinosaur names. He would sit in rapt attention, hang on to each picture, and try to blabber out the names, most of which were longer than his own.

One night, he jabbed his finger at a page and said, 'Giganotosaurus.' He hadn't even said 'Mamma' till then. That's the magic of reading aloud.

As the boys grew older, I grew weary of being a referee by day and storyteller by night. That's when their hi-tech grandmother came to the rescue. She would read out stories, record them, and turn them into podcasts for the little ones. On most nights, I was excused from their bedtime story hour.

Soon, they were reading mostly by themselves. I was relieved. But sometimes, I missed sounding ridiculous, rolling my eyes, changing voices, and watching them dissolve into giggles, eventually getting soothed into sleeping. They had grown up.

'Reading aloud is for babies,' they would say. Yet, somehow their voices lacked conviction. I ignored that. It suited me fine. They were reading on their own, which meant I could read on my own too.

A couple of years ago, I had done a storytelling session for middle-grade readers and a handful of newly minted teenagers who insisted on being a part of it. By this time, I had done several storytelling sessions with younger kids but it was unnerving to be facing older kids who would be fluent readers. What if they didn't like being read to? And what do you read to children, some of whom are avid readers, and others who hate the whole idea of reading? We tested the waters with *Lafcadio* by Shel Silverstein. Over the next few days, what I witnessed completely changed my notions about reading out loud. The children would arrive on time, grab hold of the book, and urge me to start from where we had left off the previous day. These kids were fluent with the language, and they could read independently. Yet, they loved the idea of being read to. The haters reluctantly gave in too. And soon they were fighting for the best seat in the library. I saw non-readers turning into readers, and bookworms listening for the pleasure of it.

After this, Ishaan asked me, 'How come you don't read to us anymore? It was so much fun!' I cautiously started reading to them again, once in a while.

A few months later, we collected some books and took them to Mum's place for her helper's daughters. They had just started going to school and barely knew Hindi or English. To see their eyes light up at the sight of books was joyful. I read out to them, and a few days later, I was told they were spotted buried in the books, trying to make sense of the words. Every now and then, Mum reads to them and she sees the same spark that I saw years ago in my own children. That is the power of reading out to children.

Every time a story is read aloud, a reader is born, and with every new reader, the world becomes a better place. So, read to your child, irrespective of the age, reading interest or the complete lack of it.

From picture books to chapter books, read everything. I have read labels and weather reports to my ever-eager toddlers, when unplanned vacations meant leaving behind books and toys.

I am still made to read aloud. Ten minutes and a child is all it takes for one to become a storyteller. I am a storyteller for my boys. While I narrate to them, I see their faces change. The teenage aloofness melts away, and is replaced by smiles and sparkling eyes. The books picked by them for me to read out are mostly way below the 'recommended reader level'. We march on, reading some quietly in a corner with a mug of hot chocolate, and listening to others amidst loud giggles and squeals.

Everybody Loves to Read

Both my boys and I have great love for the written word: We have cried, giggled and have been suitably scared.

There was never a conscious strategy to get the kids reading. I am sure there are methods devised for it, but mine were not based on research. I am now in the happy position that no matter what tasks I give my boys, I usually come back to find them lost in a book.

For example, bookshelf-cleaning day during the school vacations.

In the morning, the two boys report to duty and are given a five-minute lecture on their responsibilities and how I, the overworked mother, slog to keep the place clean. Two heads nod seriously and then the boys scurry across the house, collecting stray books that have magically found their way to under the sofa, on the dining table, and in all sorts of drawers, hiding between toys, socks or worse. I sigh and quietly slip out to do my round of grocery shopping or for a solitary cup of coffee.

When I step back in, I am fantasising about neat shelves with books lined up in some logical order.

In front of me is the familiar trail of books leading to two boys plonked in their favourite corners, with their noses buried in books.

'BOYS!'

A few moments pass before the sound waves reach their ears, and a few more before they are jolted back to reality. If I am lucky, the horror of the unfulfilled promise dawns upon them and they hurriedly pile the books up, making me wish I had never asked them to clean up in the first place. However, on most days they just rush to show me the book they found buried in the pile. The excitement of finding that perfect book disarms me and the next hour is spent in an animated discussion involving vampires, dragons or simply a boy.

So how did all the reading start? There were a few efforts. This is definitely not an exhaustive list of ideas—just a few things that an exasperated mum did.

HOW TO GET YOUR KID TO READ

👍 Yank out that cable

Okay, maybe not that violently but switch the damn TV off! Install child locks, bolt the room or do whatever it takes to wean her off. She need to feel bored to be able to entertain herself with stuff not involving a screen.

👍 Let your child choose

Let your child loose in the children's section of the bookstore. Allowing her to choose raises the chances of the books actually being read rather than ending up as hurriedly wrapped, last-moment birthday gifts for her friends.

👍 Be patient

'Everyone is a reader ... some just haven't found their favourite book yet.' This is especially true for kids. If a few books gather dust on the shelf, do not wince, give up and shove the remote back into their hands. Give it time. They will find their book. It is somewhat like finding the right wand before starting Hogwarts.

👍 Incentivise

Vivaan resisted books for a long time, but then we devised a game. The rules were simple—he had to read a book, tell me what it was about and get a star. Ten stars meant he got to do something he loves. Reinforcement works. Devise your own rules.

👍 Ban the banned book list

A parent once remarked that I 'should not' let the boys read *Captain Underpants*. I bought the entire series. So there.

Children get lengthy lessons on moral values at home and in school. Books need to become their sanctuary. Everything doesn't have to be informative and politically correct.

👍 Add variety

Comics, graphic novels, short stories, poetry—let your child try it all. Before you know it you might find your kid hiding in a corner guffawing at the piece of nonsense poetry he just read.

👍 Read with them

The best way to start off a child's reading journey is by

reading to her. It is also a joyful, stress-free thing to do with a child with whom you might have otherwise been fighting all day. There is absolutely no pleasure that matches bedtime reading with a small child, or a teenager, for that matter.

When the boys were younger, I used to read to them. A little later, we read together and now we just exchange notes. I love books; they love books. You cannot expect them to love something you seem to be disinterested in!

Now, every time the boys read something new, they get me to read it. They wait impatiently for me to finish, so that we can go over the jaw-dropping or tear-jerking parts again, together.

Never force

Books can never be shoved down a child's throat. I am yet to come across a parent who has successfully 'disciplined' their kid into enjoying books. So let her be. Keep motivating her, enticing her. But if in the end your child does not want to read, let her be.

Sibling fights are now usually about who gets to read the new book first, who dog-eared the pages or worse, who left the book in the washroom. The books still lie strewn all around the house and I have given up any hope of an organised bookshelf.

Inappropriate Books

'Mum, why do people kiss?'

'Umm … because they love each other?' I said, trying to disguise my nervous twitch.

'Ugh! I hate the idea of salivas mixing!'

'You might think differently in a few years,' I smiled. But then I had to know. 'Why do you ask?'

'The boy in the book I am reading, kissed a girl and was acting like buffoon about it.'

'Hmm … and how was the book?'

'Awesome!' And with that, he gave me a blow-by-blow account of the book, with only a passing mention of the awkward teen kiss.

Yes, they read books where the teen protagonists are on the threshold of adulthood. A lot of parents might label me irresponsible. If not hiding my head in the sand every time I encounter something uncomfortable makes me an irresponsible parent, then yes, I am one. The idea of broaching subjects even remotely related to sex ties lots of parents up in knots.

Children always find ways to get more information. So, banning books that fleetingly address romance never helps. Besides, they watch movies that have mild to explicit sexual or romantic undertones. Yet, similar—but much milder—content in the written form gets the book on the banned list internationally, or, at least, on the home turf. Surprisingly, children are much more forthcoming and receptive about sexual knowledge and feelings than the know-it-all adults. Only if we are more open and non-judgemental, will we be able to help our kids make somewhat intelligent choices. Actions driven by forbidden curiosity seldom lead to desirable outcomes.

Teenage years are not just about hormones and sex. There are far graver issues that plague teens. Books help them deal with infatuation, rejection, curiosity, isolation, confusion about the future, fear of failure, loss, and much more. So it is only fair that as parents we befriend all sorts of books.

As a thumb rule, I read all the books where I feel sensitive issues might be addressed. I can then tell the boys that there might be parts they find confusing, uncomfortable or plain intriguing—if so, they can talk to me about it. And believe me, they do! I feel that an honest discussion can never result in anything bad.

A few years ago, I read a book categorised as young adult. Barring one instance of an older boy kissing his girlfriend, there was nothing in the book that would make even the most conservative parent raise an eyebrow. I told Ishaan that I thought it was the kiss that pushed up its recommended reading age, since the whole premise otherwise was absolutely fine for an avid reader his age. The plot was engrossing and something I knew he would thoroughly enjoy.

'So, what do you think?' I lobbed the ball gently into his court.

'Mum, I know the whole idea behind people going out with each other. Last year most of my classmates were boasting of girlfriends. And remember, we did see a boy and girl from senior wing snogging behind the bus!'

Briefly, that protective-mommy fog swept over me and I blinked. Thankfully, he continued, 'I honestly do not feel the need for all that right now and think I need to grow up a bit more. And also, girls are annoying!'

I handed him the book and a few hours later, both of us were discussing the awesome parts in it. I would rather he experienced the excitement of reading a really great story, even if it meant he encountered the 'taboo' of a stolen kiss.

Let Them Read, Please

'I am looking for a book that inculcates good eating habits. Can you help?'

'The book that you recommended yesterday? What does it teach?'

'Indian values, I am looking for a book on our culture and values.'

These are a few of the messages that land in my inbox with alarming frequency.

Initially, I wondered if I was wrong in never seeking out the 'right' books for the boys. Maybe my choice of letting them choose, and suggesting books without considering their 'impact' was not a parent-like thing to do.

Vivaan's giggle settled the guilt. He was reading a book about a monster and his sky-high fly pie. No lesson there. Ishaan was reading a book from the Cherub series. I asked Ishaan if he learnt anything from it. He replied, 'Erm, never trust children?' An important lesson.

Most of these messages remain unanswered. But responding to people like that in the real world gets challenging. So I mostly smile and shake my head and say, 'Sorry, no idea.'

I get looked down upon. That is better than being lured into a futile argument. Arguments that mostly conclude that the useless books children read lead to aimlessness.

They are not completely off the mark. The boys are mostly aimless. They change their choice of sports every three to four months. The choice of career has varied from being a chocolate-factory taster to an astronaut to an Egyptologist. If nothing else works, there is always the lucrative option of being a toymaker. So yes, conventionally speaking, they are aimless.

Perhaps I should hold all these books and their criminal authors responsible. They are responsible for the boys being full of random ideas all the time, and being miserable when they have to wait for the next book in the series. I think I should sue these authors for giving wings to the boys' dreams, for providing them an escape route from the daily grind. And to add insult to the grave injury, the books don't even have any important lessons!

It doesn't end there. Books lie strewn all over the house, despite my threats of burning the library down. The sibling fights are mostly about books kept on the wrong shelves.

To not have a 'moral' is bad enough, but to have the word 'underpants' in the title, mention of an illegitimate baby in another, and a trail of F-words in a YA book, is unacceptable! Not only are my choices making sure that the boys grow up without morals, I am evidently also letting them learn about the unmentionable, entirely inappropriate aspects of life.

But the strange thing is that despite all these terrible influences, they are good kids. Well, as good as teenagers can possibly be. They are sensitive. They do not make friends on the basis of popularity. Their favourite workplace is a bookstore. They ask me the meanings of a dozen new words each day. And they are mostly respectful. I have never heard them use the expletives they may have read in books. In fact, these immoral books may have done more good than the moral science classes at school. They have given them an insight into the world, different cultures and themselves.

I see them buried deep within the pages, surfacing only when the real world is in dire straits, and homework completion is the only way out. Sometimes, I spot Vivaan closing the book, his thumb doubling up as a bookmark, and gazing out of the window. I wonder what is going on in that head. When I ask him, the spark returns to his eyes and he tells me, 'This book is unbelievable, Ma! You just have to take a break to thoroughly enjoy it.'

That spark prevents me from looking for a lesson. That spark makes me grateful to the author for writing the book that is now carefully clutched against his chest. There are bad words in there and possibly no lessons. It is just a great story that completely bewitched an eleven-year-old child.

So why look for a lesson? Can reading not be pursued for the sheer pleasure of it? I feel that the answer to these questions lies in our own insecurity as parents. We want to give the child the best there is—the best education, the best opportunities and the best value system. We are wary of them whiling away their time reading something that doesn't teach them anything, and abhor the idea of them picking up something that challenges our notions of right and wrong, and we imagine them copying whatever they read, blindly.

As parents, we need to sit back and stop looking for lessons in everything around us. Because what we do not realise—perhaps refuse to acknowledge—is that no lesson that is shoved in our faces is learnt, or even noticed.

If all that your child wants to do is read what he loves, not critique it or talk about his favourite character or what the story taught him, let him do that. Let him enter the world as he wishes, experience its joys, sorrows, fears and thrills and ponder over it if he so wishes. If you are lucky, he'll come and chew your brains out about it later. If not, find peace in the fact that he is reading, even if it is a useless comic, pointless science fiction, or a particularly violent series. He is reading. He is creating his own world. Let him be. He is all right.

Keep Calm and Mommy On

'Mumma. This is it. I can't go on like this. You have to cancel the homework for today! I can't concentrate with your younger son hovering over my head, and I hate maths anyway. I will become something that doesn't require maths. Why can't I leave maths?'

'Quick!' My mind was telling me to find the nearest sandpit to bury my head in. Thankfully, the sandpit found me! A student came running to call me back to the mic—the senior co-host was missing me. I hung up on Ishaan amidst vehement protests, and completely sidestepped a serious debate on non-mathematical career choices.

That night, like others, ended with an exhausted mom, with hair greying faster than the garden chameleon changes colours, a disgruntled boy who felt entirely unlucky and denied of all his 'rights', and a father's distant, self-endangering statement about the mom being too strict. And the second son silently taking notes for future reference.

Each night, when the entire household is asleep, the dogs snoring away, the fish gracefully swimming in their tank, the boys sprawled on their beds, I do the last round tucking them all in. I linger on near my older son, give him an extra kiss, and just sit there and stare. I stare at this six-foot boy, who considers himself a revolutionary in the morning, an oppressed, unfortunate boy in the afternoon, and is too exhausted to think anything by night.

The mum in me frantically looks for the tiny bundle that she had carried home from the hospital two days after he came into this world, with the tiny fingers that wrapped around hers, the big round eyes that forever followed his lifeline. All I see in that snoring face is a fledgling—sprouting wings, trying to take to the sky—who sees me as holding him back. Whatever happened to my tiny little baby?

The questions hang in balance: 'Where the hell is my baby? What do I do? Where am I going wrong?' There is no answer. For all the mothers (and fathers) out there: Do nothing. Just wait for the storm to pass! And wrong? Are you kidding me? We are the best things that could have happened to our respective families. It's just a phase, which shall pass, and transform into a storm much bigger than this, so brace yourself for the ride ahead! The baby is in there somewhere, or so we fool ourselves. Do what you do best—love unconditionally and breathe deeply. You just might make it without a trip to the shrink!

And remember, you are a mom, their best bet. You are nothing more and nothing less. You have flaws and you have strengths—they make you, define you. You are the best already. Anyone asking for an upgrade ought to be deleted from your life. You are a Supermom. Try asking the kids and they will show you the cape that flows behind your back.

Endnotes

Dealing with Diversity

1. S.K. Kang and M. Inzlicht, 'Stigma Building Blocks', *Personality and Social Psychology Bulletin, 38*(3), 357-369 (2012).

Should Religion Be a Choice?

2. Adman Preet K.S. Bedi (https://www.facebook.com/pbedi/posts/10152546120884034)

Building Resilience

3. M.E.P. Seligman, A.C. Parks and T. Steen, 'A Balanced Psychology and a Full Life', *Philosophical Transactions of the Royal Society Biological Sciences,* 359 (1449), 1379-81 (2004).
4. http://www.viacharacter.org/www/character-strengths-survey

A Million Shades of Grey

5. V. Voon, T.B. Mole, P. Banca, L. Porter Morris, S. Mitchell et al., 'Neural Correlates of Sexual Cue Reactivity in Individuals with and without Compulsive Sexual Behaviours', *PLoS ONE 9(7): e102419* (2014).

Friendship across Genders

6. K.K. Powlishta, 'The Effect of Target Age on the Activation of Genger Stereotypes, *Sex Roles,* 42, 271-282 (2000).

Of White Lies and Boring Truths

7. V. Talwar and A. Crossman, 'From Little White Lies to Filthy Liars', *Advances in Child Development and Behaviour*, 40, 139-179 (2011).

Do Nothing This Vacation!

8. Emma Seppala, *The Happiness Track: How to Apply the Science of Happiness to Accelerate Your Success* (2016).

So You Want To Be A Tiger Mom?

9. Martin E.P. Seligman, *Authentic Happiness: Using the New Positive Psychology to Realize Your Potential for Lasting Fulfilment* (2002).

Needs vs Wants

10. Bernardo J. Carducci, 'Basic Processes of Mischel's Cognitive-Affective Perspective: Delay of Gratification and Conditions of Behavioral Consistency', *The Psychology of Personality: Viewpoints, Research, and Applications*, 443–4 (2009).

Acknowledgments

A book is rarely a solitary journey and this one had a truckload of people cheering me on. First of all, none of it would have been possible without the platypuses—Anushka, Sayoni and Ayushi. They first prodded me out of the closet, got me to write, and then made this into a book. No words can sufficiently thank you all.

I have friends who mail and message at unearthly hours, reminding me to write. They read what I send, ruthlessly critique it, and believe in me more than I ever have. Without their faith, I'd never have written a single coherent sentence. And if I name one, rest will bury me at least eight feet under. Alive.

My English teacher, Mrs Mala Kohli, is a perfect example of what wonderful teachers can do. She got me to fall in love with words.

Lastly, my parents and my husband Ajay, for being the only people who are convinced that I am a bestselling author.

Dr Tanu Shree Singh has a PhD in Positive Psychology and is a lecturer in psychology. She is also struggling to be a librarian at the Reading Raccoons Library that she has set up at Faridabad. Most of her theories of bringing up children, however, have been violently challenged and reshaped by her two teenaged sons. She is surrounded by three clueless men (one by virtue of wedlock and two by virtue of the womb) and six dogs with distinct non-canine personalities, and has an ever-growing bookshelf to hide behind.